ERIC S. NOYA

THE THEATRE

AN INTRODUCTION

FOURTH EDITION

Oscar G. Brockett

HOLT, RINEHART AND WINSTON
New York   Chicago   San Francisco   Atlanta   Dallas
Montreal   Toronto

Library of Congress Cataloging in Publication Data
Brockett, Oscar Gross
    The theatre: an introduction

    Bibliography
    Includes index
    1. Theatre — History.   2. Drama — History and criticism.
3. Theatre — United States.   I. Title
PN2101.B7   1979   792   78-11850
ISBN 0-03-021676-1

Printed in the United States of America
0 1 2   008   9 8 7 6 5 4 3

To
MARK

PART 1
BASIC PROBLEMS AND THEORETICAL FOUNDATIONS

1
The Theatre as a Form of Art

The theatre is so old that its origins are lost in prehistory. When human records began, people were already performing rituals which involved most of the elements required for a fully developed theatre: a performance space, performers, action, masks or makeup, costumes, music, dance, and an audience. The function of these early rites was only partially dramatic, however, since they were usually addressed to those supernatural powers thought to control the return of spring, success in hunt and war, or the fertility of human beings and their environment. Only gradually did theatre pass out of this ritualistic phase and become an activity prized for itself. Nevertheless, it was probably in these rites that theatre had its beginnings, although it may also have stemmed in part from other impulses, such as human beings' love of storytelling and imitation.

Though its origins may be shadowy, the theatre has been with us in some form throughout human history. At times it has been highly developed and highly prized; at others it has been reduced to little more than a skeleton existing on the fringes of respectability. It has as often been

3

Primitive ritual drama in New Guinea. The two male dancers portray the sun and the moon, respectively, a pair of brothers who are both competitors and allies. (Photo by David Gillison).

denounced as praised, and its value—even its right to exist—has frequently been questioned.

During most of its existence the theatre has had to contend with constrasting responses: it has been consumed as an attractive delicacy even as it has been accused of being a distraction from more important activities. This ambivalence has been encouraged in part by theatrical terminology (such as *play, show,* and *acting*) which suggests that theatre is the product of grown-ups who have prolonged their childhood by dressing up and playing games to divert themselves and others. On the other hand, in most periods theatre has been considered by at least some segments of society to be one of the most effective tools available to human beings in their attempts to understand themselves and their world. In the twentieth century it has been accepted as a legitimate field of study in university curricula along with other more traditional subjects.

The theatre, then, has had both its detractors and its strong advocates. Nevertheless, those who value it often find themselves on the defensive with those who question whether it has any valid place in a college curriculum or whether a world dominated by film and television would miss it if it were to disappear altogether.

The Basic Elements of Theatre

One reason for varying responses can be found in the theatre's complexity and diversity. These characteristics can be seen, first of all, in the basic elements of the theatre: What is performed (script, scenario, or plan); the performance (including all the processes involved in preparation and presentation); the product (a combination of the first two ingredients); and the audience (the perceivers). Each affects conceptions of the whole—the theatre.

What Is Performed

The material performed may be extremely varied, running a gamut from variety acts to Shakespearean tragedy. An entertainer may sing a song, play music on an instrument, dance, turn cartwheels, or juggle; one or more performers may improvise a situation or several actors [1] may present a complex script. Any or all of these events may occur in a place we call a theatre. Probably for this reason, we have great difficulty in defining precisely what is meant by theatre or in specifying where theatre ceases and some other type of activity begins.

Although variety entertainment is often labeled theatrical, most frequently theatre is thought to involve some degree of storytelling or impersonation. Most typically it utilizes a written text. Nevertheless, theatre does not necessarily require a script or dialogue. But, even if variety entertainment were ruled out and our conception of theatre restricted to material in some degree dramatic, we would still be faced with great diversity, for dramatic entertainments may range through improvised scenes, pantomimes, vaudeville sketches, musical plays, and spoken dramas. Furthermore, they may be brief or lengthy; they may deal with the commonplace or the unusual, the comic or the serious. With so much diversity, it is not surprising that attitudes about the theatre vary markedly, or that some people conceive of theatre almost entirely as popular entertainment whereas others discount this aspect and find the essence of theatre in its capacity to offer penetrating insights into humanity and the world. In both instances, a part has been substituted for the whole.

Despite the great range of theatre, its history is often treated as though it were synonymous with the development of drama. Although it may distort the truth, such an approach is partially justified, for it is through the written drama that we gain our clearest impressions of the theatre of the past. It is the play script which comes down to us most nearly unchanged,

[1] The use of *actor, he, him,* and *his* to refer to indefinite sex or to groups composed of both sexes is done for convenience in the writing of this book and is not to be thought of as a sign of sexism.

while we know the other theatre arts only through such secondhand records as descriptions of the acting or pictures of single scenes.

The history of the theatre is usually constructed around drama for still another important reason: the play script forms a bridge between our values and those of the past. We are able to appreciate and understand other eras only when we find in them ideas and attitudes that have meaning today, for we remain untouched by what has no relevance to ourselves. The theatre arts of the past, when viewed in isolation from drama, may seem totally disconnected from the present, but the great plays of other times create points of contact with the feelings, the thought, and life of these periods. This common bond can then serve as a bridge to an understanding of the other theatre arts in past eras.

In recent years, however, there have been attempts to debunk the importance of language and the written script and to locate the true theatrical tradition in various kinds of popular entertainment such as circus, vaudeville, improvisation, music and dance, pantomime, and Italian *com-*

Scene from the Arena Stage production of Raisin, *a musical version of* Raisin in the Sun, *performed during the 1972-1973 season. Joe Norton (left) and Ralph Carter.* (Photo by Martha Swope.)

media dell'arte—forms admired for their immediacy of contact with audiences and for their emphasis upon visual and nonverbal aural techniques. These attempts remind us that theatrical performances need not utilize a written script or dialogue in order to be effective. Similarly, a written script may be divorced from theatrical performance and be considered a form of literature. Thus, it is possible to view theatre and drama as two separate arts, often but not always working in conjunction. But in this book drama will be treated as one of the arts of the theatre—that concerned with creating a scenario, overall plan, or complete script (including all dialogue and directions for action and stage effects) as a basis for performance, which may or may not achieve literary excellence. In this sense, drama is basic to the theatre, since virtually every performance follows a preconceived plan of some sort, however vague it may be in some cases.

Performance Processes

The second element, the processes leading up to and involved in performance, gives concreteness to what is presented by translating the potential of a script, scenario, or plan into actuality. A performance normally requires the cooperation and creative efforts of many persons: playwright, actors, director, designers, technicians, dancers, musicians, publicists, and all others involved in conceiving, preparing, presenting, and marketing a production.

The number of persons involved in this process varies widely. In the earliest theatrical performances all artistic functions were often served by one person, but gradually specialists emerged and the various theatre arts were separated. The actor and the playwright attained reognition first, probably because their functions are basic and closely allied. Since drama tells its story and presents its conflicts primarily through the speeches and actions of characters, it assumes the existence of actors who will lend their bodies and voices for the time needed to play out the drama.

The actor and the playwright are by necessity complementary, since each needs the other for the completion of his art. The actor may practice his profession without the aid of the playwright, for he may compose or improvise his own speech and action—that is, he may become his own dramatist—but unless his improvisation achieves a high degree of excellence, it will not long command attention. To hold interest, a performance must, as a rule, be organized to tell a story, reveal a character, illustrate an idea, or build interest in other ways. As the length of the performance increases, so does the need to interweave story, character, and ideas, or to provide complex appeals of other kinds. As these demands are met successfully, the actor approaches more and more the function of the playwright. On the other hand, the person best able to construct an interesting series of events is not necessarily the one most able to enact these events for an audience. Thus, the specialized demands made upon the actor and the playwright have led to separate, though closely related, professions.

Although the playwright and the actor are probably most dependent on each other, they clearly benefit from the assistance of directors, designers, musicians, dancers, and others. The need for the director arises as soon as more than one actor is involved, since someone must mediate the differences of opinion about interpretation of roles, lines, or the entire script and about positions and activities on the stage. However, the director is more than a mediator: he is responsible for envisioning the production as a whole and for designing, editing, and coordinating stage action with the visual background, costumes, lights, music, and dance.

The director, therefore, is involved in many artistic decisions about his productions. In permanent companies someone must also be concerned with maintaining artistic excellence in all the productions, each of which may be staged by a different director. Therefore, many companies appoint an artistic director to oversee all artistic processes and to uphold a high standard of production. In addition, most European companies employ a dramaturg (or literary adviser) whose responsibilities include seeking out and recommending plays for production, adapting scripts as needed, making sure that appropriate research is done and made available to the company's directors, and other matters that relate to the selection and interpretation of the repertory. The dramaturg, now just beginning to be known in this country, seems likely to become an accepted member of American companies.

The various elements that go into a production are usually contributed by separate artists. The visual background, for example, is the work of

Some contemporary companies are primarily concerned with visual images, rather than the spoken text. The Bird Hoffman Foundation's production of Einstein on the Beach *in 1976 is an example of this school. Directed by Robert Wilson and Philipp Lelan. (Photo ©1976 by Babette Mangolte.)*

the set, lighting, and costume designers, who seek to interpret the qualities found in the script through visual means. The scenic designer not only indicates place and historical period, he also supplies the architectural forms, light and shadow, colors, line, and composition which interpret, add to, or reflect the drama's action. In like manner, the costumer, the lighting designer, and the choreographer seek to embody the mood and spirit of a play through visual means. Still other personnel are needed to carry out the plans of the designers, to publicize the production, to sell tickets, and to make sure that the theatre operates efficiently. (All of these processes will be discussed at length later in this book.)

The Product

What the audience sees when it goes to the theatre—the performance—is a meshing of script or plan with theatrical processes. The result may be divided into two broad (though admittedly oversimplified) categories: *popular entertainment* and *theatre as an art form*. The two may and often do overlap, and liking one does not necessarily mean disliking the other, although audiences often seem to divide along these lines.

As the term implies, popular entertainment seeks primarily to provide diversion for a mass audience. It draws on (either consciously or unconsciously) the dominant attitudes, prejudices, and interests of the day; it usually employs easily recognizable (even stereotyped) characters, situa-

Godspell is an example of theatre as popular entertainment. Conceived and directed by John-Michael Tebelak. (Photo by Martha Swope.)

tions, and theatrical conventions, while manipulating them with sufficient novelty to be entertaining but usually without offering important new perceptions or raising any disturbing questions that challenge the audience's views. Because it intends primarily to provide diversion, it can easily be grouped with games, sports, and other recreational pastimes. This is not to imply that recreation for large numbers of people is not an important function, for to divert audiences from their cares and to offer release from the routine of existence is to provide an important service, both psychologically and sociologically. Nor is it meant to suggest that theatre need not be entertaining, for if it cannot capture and hold attention, it cannot command a following. Nevertheless, if what happens in theatre is only recreational or entertaining and does not offer any additional appeals, it may be (and often is) dismissed as lacking in true significance.

What Is Art? A complete picture of the theatre demands that it also be looked at as one of the arts. But first it is important to review briefly some answers that have been given to the question: What is art? Probably no term has been discussed so frequently or defined so ambiguously. Until the eighteenth century, *art* was used almost always to designate the systematic application of knowledge or skill to achieve some predetermined result. The word is still used in that sense when we speak of the art (or craft) of medicine, politics, or persuasion. During the eighteenth century it became customary to divide the arts into two groups, "useful" and

Scene from an adaptation of Maxim Gorky's novel The Last Ones *as staged at the Prague National Theatre in 1966. Directed by Alfred Radok. The action occurred in three different planes and was accompanied by still projections or films. Setting by Josef Svoboda. (Photo copyright by Jaromir Svoboda. Courtesy Joseph Svoboda.)*

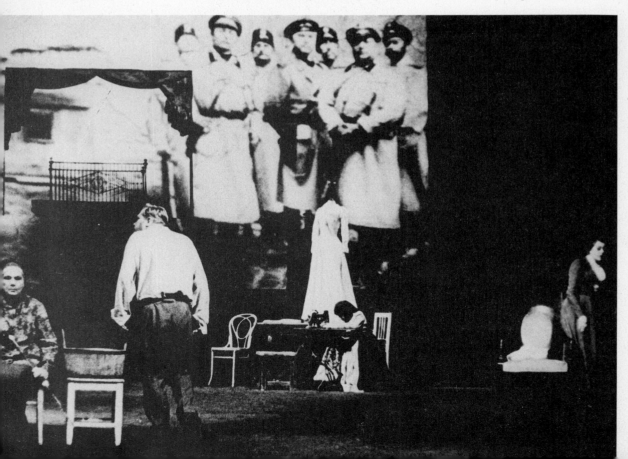

"fine." Into the latter category were placed literature, painting, sculpture, architecture, music, and dance. At the same time the idea arose that while the useful arts may easily be taught and mastered, the fine arts, as products of genius, cannot be reduced to rules or principles that can be learned. As a result, since about 1800 art has often been depicted as too lofty to be fully understandable. Many critics also have implied that only those with truly superior sensitivity can fully appreciate art and that the average person mistakes some inferior product for authentic artistic expression. Thus, those who think of theatre as an art form are often at odds with those who think of it as "show business."

If no definition of art is universally accepted, some of its distinguishing characteristics can be explored by comparing it with other approaches to experience. First and most broadly, art is one way whereby man seeks to understand the world. In this respect, it may be compared with history, philosophy, or science, each of which strives to discover and record patterns in human experience. All of these approaches recognize that human experience is composed of innumerable happenings which have occurred to an infinite number of people through countless generations, and that each person's life is made up of a series of momentary occurrences, many seeming to come about wholly by chance. One question they seek to answer is: What significant patterns can be perceived behind the apparent randomness? The search for meaning may take a different tack in each field, but it is always directed toward discovering those relationships that reveal order within what would otherwise seem to be chance events. Art, then, as one approach, shapes perceptions about human experience into forms (or patterned relationships) that help us order our views about humankind and the universe.

There are, however, significant differences in the methods used in various approaches to human experience. Historian, philosopher, and scientist do their research and then attempt to set down their conclusions in logical, expository prose; a point of view is expressed and proof marshaled to support that view and to gain its acceptance. They direct their appeal primarily to the intellect. The artist, on the other hand, works primarily from his own perceptions and seeks to involve the audience's emotions, imagination, and intellect directly. A playwright consequently presents events as though they are occurring at that moment before our eyes; we absorb them in the way we absorb life itself—through their direct operation on our senses. Thus, as art differs from life by stripping away irrelevant details and organizing events to compose a connected pattern, so a play illuminates and comments (though sometimes indirectly) on human experience even as it seemingly creates human experience.

But, just as we do not mistake a statue for a real person, we do not mistake stage action for reality. Rather, we usually view a play with what Samuel Taylor Coleridge called a "willing suspension of disbelief." By this concept he meant that, while we know the events of a play are not real, we agree for the moment not to disbelieve their reality. We are nevertheless not usually moved to immediate action by what we see on the stage as we would be by real-life events. We watch one man seemingly kill another, but make no attempt to rescue the victim or to call the police. This state in which we are sufficiently detached to view an artistic event semiobjectively is sometimes called *esthetic distance*. At the same time, the distance must not be so great as to induce indifference. Therefore, while a degree of detachment is necessary, involvement is of equal importance. This feeling of kinship is sometimes called *empathy*. Thus, we watch a play with a double sense of concern and detachment. It is both a removed and an intensified reaction of a kind seldom possible outside esthetic experience. Another way of putting this is that art (that is, a statue, a musical composition, or a drama) lifts us above the everyday fray and gives us something like a "god's-eye" view of human experience.

Some attributes of art, then, are these: Art always attempts to epitomize life. It is one method through which we may discover and record patterns which provide insights, perceptions, and understanding about ourselves and our world, and thus is one form of knowledge. In addition, art is an imaginative reshaping of experience which operates directly on our senses in a way that involves us both esthetically and empathically, allowing us to be simultaneously at a distance from and involved in the experience so that we participate in it emotionally even as we gain from it new intellectual insights. Art lays claim, then, to being serious (in the sense of having something important to communicate), but because its methods are so indirect (it presents experience but does not attempt to explain it fully) it is often ambiguous and therefore may easily be misunderstood.

Special Attributes of Theatre as an Art. Even within the fine arts theatre holds a special place; it is the art that comes closest to life as it is lived from day to day. Not only is human experience and action its subject, it also uses live human beings (actors) as its primary means of communicating with an audience. Quite often the speech of the performers approximates that heard in real life; the actors may wear costumes that might be seen on the street; and they may perform in settings that recall actual places. Not all theatre attempts to be so realistic and at times it may even approximate other performing arts (such as dance and music), but nevertheless it is the art most capable of recreating man's typical experiences.

Such lifelikeness is also one of the reasons theatre is often insufficiently valued: a play, a setting, the acting may so resemble what is familiar to spectators that they fail to recognize how difficult it is to produce this lifelikeness skillfully. To a certain degree all people are actors; they vary the roles they play (almost moment by moment) according to the people they encounter. In doing so, they utilize the same tools as the actor: voice, speech, movement, gesture, psychological motivation, and the like. Consequently, most persons do not fully recognize the problems faced by a skilled actor. Even those within the theatre often differ in their opinions about whether artistic excellence depends primarily on talent and instinct or on training and discipline.

Theatre further resembles life in being ephemeral. As in life, each episode is experienced and then immediately becomes part of the past. When the performance ends, its essence can never be fully recaptured. Unlike a novel, painting, or statute, each of which remains relatively unchanged, a theatrical production when it is ended lives only in the play script, program, pictures, reviews, and memories of those who were present.

Theatre resembles life also in being the most objective of the arts, since characteristically it presents both outer and inner experience through speech and action. As in life, it is through listening and watching that we come to know characters both externally and internally. What we learn about their minds, personalities, and motivations comes from what they say and do and from what others tell us about them. Thus we absorb a theatrical performance the way we do a scene from real life.

Additionally, theatre can be said to resemble life because of the complexity of its means for, like a scene from life itself, it is made up of intermingled sound, movement, place, dress, lighting, and so on. In other words, theatre draws on all the other arts: literature in its script; painting, architecture, and sculpture (and sometimes dance) in its spectacle; and speech and music in its audible aspects. In some ways, then, theatre encompasses all the other arts.

Furthermore, theatre is psychologically the most immediate of the arts.

Theatre combines all the elements of art, as may be seen in the opening scene of Siege of Corinth *staged at the Metropolitan Opera in 1975, with Harry Theyard, Beverly Sills, and Justine Diaz. (Courtesy of the Metropolitan Opera Archives.)*

Several contemporary critics have argued that the essence of theatre—what distinguishes it from other dramatic media such as television and film—lies in the simultaneous presence of live actors and spectators in the same room, and that everything else is expendable. On the surface, theatre may seem to have several drawbacks when compared with other media. For example, more people often see a filmed or televised show on a single evening than can attend a live production during an entire year. In fact, theatre may be likened to a handcrafted product in an age of mass production. Thousands of copies of a film may be printed and shown throughout the world simultaneously and year after year, and a televised program may be videotaped and repeated at will. These media, too, may make performers world-famous almost overnight, whereas the actor in the theatre may build up an international reputation only over a considerable period of time.

Nevertheless, a live performance has important attributes that television and film cannot duplicate. The most significant of these are the three-dimensionality of the theatrical experience and the special relationship between performers and spectators. In film and television, the camera is used to select what the audience can see and to ensure that it will see nothing more; in the theatre, on the other hand, since the full acting area remains visible, the audience may choose what it will watch, even though the director may attempt to focus attention on some specific aspect of a scene. Perhaps most important, during a live performance there is continuous interaction between performer and spectator; even as the actor is eliciting responses from the audience, those responses in turn are affecting the actor's performance. Thus, a live performance permits the audience a far more active role than television and film do. Ultimately, there is a fundamental difference in the psychological responses aroused by electronic media and theatre because the former presents pictures of events whereas the latter performs the actual events in what amounts to the same space as that occupied by the audience. This difference results in one unique characteristic of theatre: its ability to offer intense sensory experience through the simultaneous presence of live actors and audience.

It is to these special qualities—lifelikeness, ephemerality, objectivity, complexity, and psychological immediacy—that we can relate both the weaknesses and strengths of theatre.

The Audience

The fourth basic element of theatre is the audience, because until the public sees the material performed we usually do not call it theatre. For all the arts a public is imperative, but for most this public may be thought of as individuals—the reader of a novel or poem, the viewer of a painting or a piece of sculpture—each of whom may experience the

William Hogarth's The Laugh-
ing Pit, *showing spectators in the
pit, men of fashion and orange
girls in the boxes, musicians in the
orchestra pit. Note the spikes to
prevent spectators from climbing
onto the stage, and the candles on
the front of the boxes. (From an
eighteenth-century engraving.
Courtesy of the University of
Iowa Library.)*

work in isolation. But a theatre audience is assembled as a group at a
given time and place to experience a performance.

Why Does an Audience Attend the Theatre? One of the most powerful
motives for going to the theatre is the desire for *entertainment,* which
implies suspension of personal cares, relaxation of tensions, and a feeling
of well-being, satisfaction, and renewal. But although everyone may
believe that the theatre should provide entertainment, not all agree on
what is entertaining. Many would exclude any treatment of controversial
subject matter on the grounds that an audience goes to the theatre to
escape from cares rather than to be confronted with problems. This attitude is frequently labeled the "tired businessman's" approach, and it is
sometimes charged that the Broadway theatre is merely a place to relax
after a hard day's work, a spot to take prospective clients to put them in
the proper frame of mind for business dealings, or an attraction for out-
of-town tourists who are looking for another sight to see.

Other persons look to theatre for *stimulation.* They too desire to be
entertained, but argue that the theatre should also provide new insights
and provocative perceptions about significant topics, advocate action

about political and social issues, or increase awareness of and sensitivity to others and surroundings. This audience is inclined to view "theatre-as-recreation" as a debasement of art. Both points of view are valid in part, but adherents of neither point of view should attempt to limit unduly the theatre's offerings. The whole range of drama should be available to audiences, for the health of the theatre depends upon breadth of appeal.

In America today the success of a play is frequently judged by its ability to attract large audiences over a considerable period of time. But is a play to be considered a failure if it does not achieve financial success? Not necessarily. A dramatist has a right to select his audience just as much as an audience has to select a play. Actually, he does so when he chooses his subject matter, characters, and techniques, for, consciously or unconsciously, he has an ideal spectator in mind. Although he may hope for universal acceptance, he desires the favorable response of a particular group. Consequently, a play may be deemed successful if it achieves the desired response from the audience for which it was primarily intended. It is sometimes forgotten that there are many levels of taste and that the same play is unlikely to appeal to them all. Nevertheless, most American theatres have been operated on the premise that public taste is uniform or that the only valid taste is that of the majority. Until recently little was done to meet the needs of minority audiences, although Off-Broadway, Off-Off-Broadway, regional, and university theatres are doing much to remedy this situation.

Financial Support and Theatrical Programming. If a theatre is to survive it must be concerned with its ticket sales unless financial support is available from other sources. In America there was until recently an almost superstitious faith in the box office as the only acceptable means of support on the grounds that if money is accepted from any other source, freedom of expression would surely be lost. Advocates of this view admit that a theatre which depends solely upon box office receipts is at the mercy of public whim, but they either see this as healthy or as the best of the alternatives. Advocates of a more diversified theatre usually point to Europe, where most governments—both national and local—appropriate money each year to subsidize the theatre. In most cases, these subsidies have not led to undue interference in the affairs of the theatres (although this is no valid argument that they could not in America).

The purposes of a subsidy may be several. First, it acts as a cushion against failure and relieves the theatre from the need to make a commercial success of each production. Second, it enables a theatre to sell tickets at a lower cost and to make productions available to a larger proportion of the population. Third, it normally provides support for a permanent company that produces a cross-section of drama for a wide range of tastes. Fourth, it encourages concern for theatre as an art form by providing support for imaginative plays and experimental productions that might not appeal to a large audience.

In America, subsidies have normally taken the form of grants from philanthropic foundations or gifts from private groups or individuals. But in 1965 the government took a step toward acknowledging its responsibility to the arts when federal legislation established the National Endowment for the Arts to make grants of appropriated funds to groups or projects with considerable potential for growth and audience appeal. Since then federal appropriations have steadily increased, although they are still small in proportion to the country's population. The federal government has also encouraged each state to establish an arts council, and consequently most states now have official bodies charged with assisting and encouraging the arts.

Although American federal and state agencies now give financial assistance to a number of theatre groups, their approach still differs markedly from European practices. First, in Europe governments have long taken it for granted that the arts should be subsidized by the state just as public education, museums, and libraries are, for they consider the cultural well-being of their citizens a continuation of the educational opportunities provided children. Second, in Europe governmental units often own or lease the theatre buildings used by the companies they subsidize and thus they provide companies with permanent and well-equipped facilities. This arrangement may exist at any of three levels: national, state, or municipal. Third, and perhaps most important, in Europe once a company has been awarded state support, it thereafter continues (except in rare cases) to receive it. Therefore, it can make long-range plans with

A nineteenth-century vaudeville, performed by the Prince Imperial and courtiers at the Tuileries, Paris, c. 1869. (Culver Pictures.)

confidence. In America, on the contrary, many companies have been given strong initial support only to have it withdrawn after a few years on the grounds that they should now be able to support themselves, thereby perpetuating the idea that if art cannot establish itself as a business it does not deserve to survive. Furthermore, in America, government agencies that grant subsidies do not know more than one or two years in advance whether they will have funds to assist theatres, since their own budgets depend on legislative appropriations which may vary radically from year to year. Nevertheless, in terms of financial support, American theatres now fare much better than in the past.

Although government subsidy of theatre in America is still small, other types of subsidies (often indirect or hidden) are common. Almost all educational theatres in America operate in rent-free buildings and with staffs paid from funds other than ticket sales. (It is often said that universities are the major patrons of the arts in America.) Community theatres are subsidized by the voluntary labor of members, and some receive financial help from local governments as well. Many professional theatres outside of New York receive aid from philanthropic foundations. Only the commercial theatre in New York tends to depend exclusively on box office receipts for its support. Regardless of source, however, financial support is necessary, and audiences affect the kinds of plays presented in proportion to a theatre's dependence upon their patronage for its income.

The Audience's Expectations and Theatrical Offerings. Audiences also affect the theatre through their expectations. They become accustomed to certain techniques and subject matter and quite frequently resist change. Audiences do not reject all changes, however, for they have flocked to new modes of musical comedy and have welcomed many new approaches to production.

Audiences (like all human beings) resist what they do not understand. In the late nineteenth century, Ibsen (now usually called the founder of modern drama) was denounced by critics and audiences, and his plays were forbidden production in many countries. To spectators of the time, Ibsen's plays seemed to advocate immoral actions and to deal with subjects unsuitable for public discussion. To understand the uproar, however, one need only recall similar responses in the late 1960s when such works as *Hair* introduced nudity, obscenity, rock music, and a new life style as significant dramatic ingredients.

Audiences probably wish to encounter novel experiences, but as a rule they want the new to be presented through familiar theatrical conventions and within acceptable moral limits. Any extreme break with custom is apt to be resisted by the majority until the innovations no longer seem baffling. On the other hand, during the 1960s a new, younger, and more adventurous audience greeted almost every innovation with enthusiasm. But by the late 1970s audiences were showing signs of a new conservatism.

Whatever its response, the audience does influence the choice of plays, for a producer must keep in mind the tastes of potential ticket buyers.

Unless he can attract spectators in sufficient numbers, he cannot long survive in the theatre. Each producer may cater to a different type of spectator or level of taste, but how that audience responds to each new production helps to determine what it will be offered in the future.

The Physical Presence of the Audience. The audience also affects the theatre through its powerful psychological impact upon performers. Actors both crave and fear audiences. Many are subject to severe "stage fright" before a performance begins, only to become at ease when they step onto the stage. Almost all are "keyed up" because of uncertainty about the reception they will be given. Fortunately, most actors use this alertness to advantage during performance. The audience, in its turn, responds to stimuli received from the production, and its reactions (in the form of rapt attention, restlessness, laughter, silence when laughter is expected) clearly affect the performers. Thus, there is a constant interchange between actor and audience.

The responses of an audience serve either to reward or to punish. Favorable response can inspire an actor to do his finest work, while unfavorable reactions may reduce him to uncertainty and clumsiness. Each actor, however, tends to respond differently. For example, one performer in a comedy which is not receiving the anticipated laughter may relapse into a mechanical delivery of lines, while another may exert himself ever more strenuously until he elicits laughter, even if he must resort to completely inappropriate means. Some actors are tempted to enlarge upon anything that seems to gain audience approval, while others appear incapable of initiative even in the face of an emergency. Because of "overacting" or "underacting" induced by the audience, productions often take on a tone quite different from that intended.

The "psychology of the audience" is a fascinating but little understood subject. Nevertheless, it plays a significant role in every performance, for not all of the audience's reactions can be attributed to the production. The mood in which it comes to the theatre is important. Since for many individuals attendance at the theatre is a special occasion, there may be an atmosphere of festivity which determines initial responses. Conditions that affect the audience's comfort, such as ventilation, lighting, and type of seating, also influence reactions, as do the size of the auditorium, the closeness to the performers, and the arrangement of seating in relation to the stage. Perhaps most important, individuals are transformed into a group by being placed in close physical proximity and by sharing an experience. It has long been known that a small audience scattered through a large auditorium will not laugh as readily as the same number seated together. Community of response, then, influences both the spectators and the actors.

During the 1960s interest in the audience's role was especially strong. Both Joseph Chaikin of the Open Theatre and Jerzy Grotowski of the Polish Laboratory Theatre argued that the essence of the theatre lies in the simultaneous presence of live actors and spectators in the same

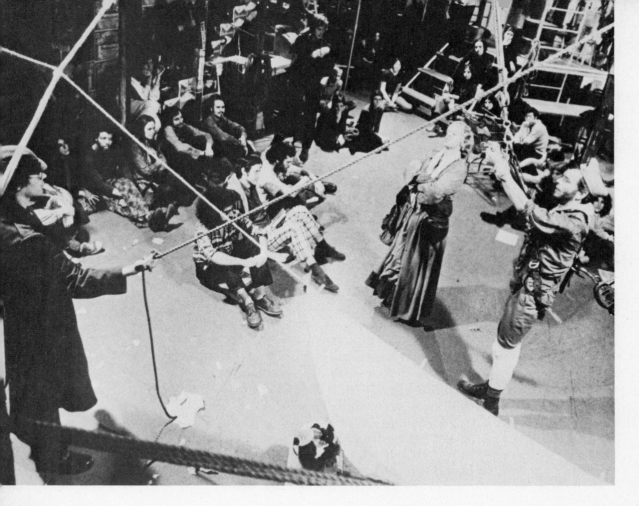

In a setting that breaks down traditional barriers, actors and audience share performance space in the Performance Group production of Mother Courage and Her Children *by Bertolt Brecht. (Courtesy of The Performance Group.)*

room, and that everything except this relationship is expendable. Richard Schechner, advocating "environmental" theatre, argued that the audience must be considered "scene-makers" as well as "scene-watchers," for they are part of the total picture even if they are unaware of it. He went on to declare that the entire theatrical space should be used by both actors and audience. The Living Theatre went even further and sought to involve the audience directly in the action of their pieces and to break down all distinctions between spectators and performers.

Many of these innovations grew out of the desire to make spectators feel more directly involved in performances by eliminating traditional barriers. But reducing the physical distance between actor and spectator does not necessarily increase the sense of involvement. In fact, Grotowski charged that the Living Theatre's approach alienated audiences by reducing esthetic distance and making the spectators feel self-conscious. He argued that the proper solution lies in deciding what role the audience should play in each production and then designing the physical space so they will be induced to play that role without being aware of it. It is difficult to assess the ultimate importance of these experiments, but they are significant for seeking to manipulate the audience–actor physical relationship (as a major element in every theatrical performance) to achieve a more powerful and meaningful response.

The Problem of Value

The four basic elements of theatre—script, process, product, and audience—may come together in almost infinite combinations and with equally diverse results. We should be willing to acknowledge that not all theatre is likely to appeal to all segments of the public and that responses to it are almost inescapably varied. The concern of this book is primarily the *theatre* as a form of art.

Despite all one can say about it, however, the nature and value of art are still not widely understood by the general public. In a society preoccupied with material success, as ours has been, art does not appear to be very useful, since it does not produce such obvious benefits as those of medicine or engineering. Even those artists (including performers) who are widely known and accepted are usually admired more for their commercial success than for their artistic talents, having shown that they can compete in the business world. Generally, careers in the arts are considered highly risky because they seldom offer financial security. Such attitudes about art have led to a situation in which children are systematically (although not necessarily intentionally) discouraged from developing their talents. By the time adulthood is reached, the average American has suppressed all artistic inclinations. Far too many adults are thus cut off from or are only partly aware of one of man's primary ways of knowing his world and understanding himself.

Still, it is difficult to defend art on the basis of its immediate utility. Art ultimately must be valued because of its capacity to improve the quality of life: by increasing our sensitivity to others and our surroundings, by sharpening our perceptions, by reshaping our values so that moral and societal concerns take precedence over material well-being. Of all the arts, theatre has perhaps the greatest potential as a humanizing force, for at its best it asks us to enter imaginatively into the lives of others so we may understand their aspirations and motivations. Through role-playing (either in daily life or in the theatre) we come to understand who and what we are and to see ourselves in relation to others. Perhaps most important, in a world given increasingly to violence, the value of being able to understand and feel for others as human beings cannot be overestimated, because violence flourishes most fully when we so dehumanize others that we no longer think of their hopes, aims, and sufferings but treat them as objects to be manipulated or on whom to vent our frustrations. To know (emotionally, imaginatively, and intellectually) what it

At a rehearsal of Androcles and
the Lion *in 1913, George Bernard Shaw demonstrates a point
about a fight to Harley Granville
Barker and Lillah MacCarthy.
(Courtesy Enthoven Collection,
Victoria and Albert Museum.)*

means to be human in the broadest sense ought to be one of the primary
goals of both education and life; for reaching that goal no approach has
greater potential than theatre, since humans are its subject and living
beings its primary medium.

But the theatre's great potential is not always or automatically fulfilled.
Those working in theatre often are preoccupied with the immediate process or with egotistical goals, while audiences often concentrate only on
surface qualities and students of theatre may fail to see anything in their
study of the past that is pertinent to them. Furthermore, the skill and
content of theatrical performances are not always of high quality. Natu-
rally, if theatre is to realize its potential, all concerned must be willing to
look beneath the surface and insist on excellence.

Unfortunately, quality—unlike quantity—is not measurable except sub-
jectively. And subjectivity takes us into the realm of taste, judgment,
and a host of variables about which agreement is seldom possible. There
are many levels of taste, many degrees of complexity, and a wide range of
quality. But, if we cannot expect ever to achieve complete agreement, we
all can sharpen our own perceptions of the theatre and its processes. To
do this, we need first to understand the theatre and how it works. Second,
we need to develop some approach through which we can judge the relative merits of what is performed and how it is performed. Then, we
should work to encourage those theatrical values that seem important to
us. In this way we may acquire understanding and judgment—that is, we
become criticis of the theatre.

Under present conditions, most Americans come to adulthood having
been denied extensive exposure to the arts, especially to the theatre. Prior

to entering college, few student have the opportunity to study and practice the art of the theatre in any systematic way. As an aid in compensating for this lack, the chapters that follow provide an overview of the theatre in its various aspects: how plays are structured; what critics look for; how the theatre has changed and developed through the ages; how it functions today; and how each theatre artist makes use of the materials available to him. Taken together, these discussions, it is hoped, will lay the foundation for intelligent and sensitive reactions to the theatre.

2
The Script: Dramatic Structure, Form, and Style

The play script is the typical starting point for the theatrical production. It is also the most common residue of production, since the script usually remains intact after its performance ends. Because the same script may serve as a basis for many different productions, it has greater permanence than its theatrical representations and therefore comes to be considered a literary work. Consequently, drama is often taught quite apart from theatre, and many people who read plays have never seen a live dramatic performance. Probably the majority of students get their first glimpse of theatre through the reading of plays in literature classes. But the script in itself may seem unsatisfactory or puzzling, for it is essentially a blueprint that demands from both reader and performer the imaginative recreation of much that is only implied on the printed page. Therefore, learning how to read, understand, and fill out the script (either in the mind or on the stage) is essential if the power of a play is to be fully realized.

But the beginner often does not know how to approach reading a play or watching a performance. Today, many persons experience drama almost entirely through television or film, for which no written script is usually available for reading and in which the camera has screened out all details not thought important by the director. Both reading a play and watching a live performance are quite different from watching a drama performed in an electronic medium; full appreciation of a written script or of a live performance comes only with experience in which concentration and imagination have been primary elements.

On Reading a Play

There are no rules about how one should read a play. Nevertheless, some observations may be helpful to those for whom play reading is still a new experience. First, one must accept that the ability to read imaginatively and perceptively is a basic skill needed by all persons who seek to become educated, for without it much of human experience is forever lost, and intellectually we remain children suffering from historical and cultural amnesia.

Like all writers, the dramatist in conveying his intentions must resort to symbols—letters grouped into words, words into sentences, sentences into paragraphs. If these symbols are to be intelligible, the reader must transform them into concrete images—that is, he must use his imagination to convert the symbols into objects, actions, and meanings.) His perceptions of these images must approximate those envisioned by the author when he set down the symbols. Without the reader's imagination, word symbols would remain forever inert on the page and reading would be impossible.

Since all writers do not express themselves in the same form, all written works cannot be read in the same way. Each form has its own characteristics, and each makes distinctive demands on the reader. Thus, we cannot read a play in the same way we do an historical treatise, an essay, a biography, a novel, or a poem. To read a play adequately, we must first adjust our minds to the dramatic form so that its contents may be perceived. In other words, the reader must seek to adopt the dramatic point of view (rather than the historical, essayistic, scientific, novelistic, or some other point of view).

Both writing and reading may be viewed as substitutes or alternatives to speaking and listening, for a writer sets down in words what he might communicate orally if everyone he wished ever to reach were in his presence simultaneously. A written passage is an author's way of preserving his perceptions and ideas in a form that can be communicated to others. But when he writes, he typically formulates his ideas and perceptions more precisely than when he speaks, for the spoken word is usually spontaneous, attuned to the immediate sensory responses and visible reactions

Oedipus the King as presented at Epidaurus in 1960. (Courtesy of the Greek National Theatre.)

of the auditors, and any misunderstandings can be clarified by additions or alterations. A play is distinctive in part because it is a form made up primarily of dialogue that must be constructed with great care in order to convey its intentions precisely while at the same time creating the sense of being the spontaneous oral utterances of characters involved in a developing action. Thus, it is at once a highly formal structure and a simulated spontaneous reflection of human experience.

Drama requires the reader to contribute more than any other form does. Not only must the reader see and understand what is explicitly said and done, but he must also be aware of all that is merely implied or left unsaid. While the dramatist may use stage directions to clarify setting, situation, or tone, for the most part he conveys his intentions through dialogue. Therefore, in reading a play we should assume that the writer has set down precisely what he wishes to say, but that, because he must convey his intentions through a likeness of conversation, we must be sensitive—as in real life—to the implications, unspoken feelings, and even deliberate deceptions typical of human interaction. Therefore, the reader must be alert to the nuances and shadings of each word and phrase.

It is impossible here to go through one or more plays line by line to explore the problems and pleasures of reading scripts. Rather, this book in its totality is intended to provide the kind of information and to stimulate the kind of imaginative inquiry needed to envision the mimic world of a play. Nevertheless, some of the problems can be illustrated and some approaches suggested. Take, for example, the opening lines of the oldest play that will be discussed at length in this book, Sophocles' *Oedipus the King* (a Greek tragedy written about 430 B.C. and usually considered one of the greatest dramas of all times).

OEDIPUS: My children, . . .
Why have you strewn yourselves before these altars
In supplication, with your boughs and garlands?
The breath of incense rises from the city
With a sound of prayer and lamentation.
                                        Children,
I would not have you speak through messengers,
And therefore I have come myself to hear you—
I, Oedipus, who bear the famous name.

The surviving manuscripts of this play include practically no stage directions. (Dudley Fitts and Robert Fitzgerald, the translators of the English version quoted here, have prefaced the opening scene with a descriptive passage based on what they have deduced from the dialogue and from information about Greek theatre architecture. Such added stage directions remind us that it is often necessary to reread a play several times before we become fully aware of the implications summed up in such additions, especially if the play is remote from us in time or unfamiliar in style.)

The title of Sophocles' play informs us that Oedipus is the king, and from later lines we learn that the action takes place in front of the palace. But what does this palace look like? Unless in our minds the place of the action is to remain wholly abstract we must form some image of it. We learn almost immediately that there are altars (but where are they placed and what is their physical appearance?) and that those who are assembled are praying for help (but it takes some knowledge of Greek customs to know that the boughs and garlands mentioned in the lines were symbols associated with suppliants and that the incense referred to is rising from altars dedicated to the various gods who are being entreated for mercy). Oedipus immediately assumes the role of father and protector of his subjects, for otherwise he would not address those assembled as "children" (when succeeding lines establish that the crowd ranges in age from young children to old men). The tone of Oedipus' speeches tells us that he rather self-righteously accepts the role of savior of his people. (Only as we read subsequent scenes do we gradually recognize the irony of his attitude, for he himself is the cause of the plague.) Like most plays, *Oedipus the King* immediately raises these questions: How are the characters dressed? How are they positioned? Do they move? If so, when and in what manner? At what tempo does the scene proceed? What is the tone of the scene?

Many other questions could be enumerated, but these illustrate that inwardly and imaginatively seeing and hearing a script is not a simple undertaking. Yet, it can be done adequately if we cultivate the imagination and develop the understanding appropriate to the task. Perhaps the best place to begin is with a look at how plays are constructed.

Dramatic Action

Broadly speaking, a play is a representation of man in action. But "action" does not mean mere physical movement; it involves as well the motivations (both mental and psychological) that lie behind visible behavior. "Man in action," therefore, includes the whole range of feelings, thoughts, and deeds that define what sort of creature man is—what he does and why he does it. Because the dramatic potentials of this subject are almost infinite, a single play by necessity can depict only a small part of the whole. Furthermore, because each playwright's vision and methods differ somewhat from those of others, each drama is in some respects unique. On the other hand, outstanding plays, no matter when or where they were written, tend to have qualities in common that permit us to draw conclusions about the characteristics of effective dramatic action.

Aristotle (the Greek philosopher of the fourth century B.C.) declares that a play should have a beginning, middle, and end. On the surface, this statement seems obvious and overly simple, but it summarizes a fundamental principle. Basically, it means that a play should be *complete and self-contained,* that everything necessary for understanding it should be included within the play itself. If this principle is not observed, the action will probably be confusing or unsatisfying to audiences.

Dramatic action should be *purposeful*. It should be organized so as to arouse a specific response, such as pity and fear, joy, ridicule or indignation, thoughtful contemplation, or laughter. The purpose may be simple or complex, but the events, the characters, the mood, and other elements should be shaped and controlled with some purpose in mind.

Dramatic action should be *varied*. Although the action should be unified, variety (in plot, characterization, ideas, mood, or spectacle) is also needed if monotony and predictability are to be avoided.

Dramatic action should *engage and maintain interest*. The characters must command the audience's attention, the situation must be compelling enough to arouse interest, the issues must seem vital enough to warrant concern, or the aural and visual devices must be sufficiently novel to excite and hold interest.

Dramatic action should be *probable* (that is, all of the elements should be logically consistent). Probability is what most persons have in mind when they speak of a play's believability. But probability, or believability, does not depend upon similarity to real life, for a play that depicts impossible events may be called believable if the incidents occur logically within the framework created by the playwright. (For example, in Iones-

Dramatic action should be probable. Although they are unusual, the costumes, set, and action in the Chelsea Theatre production of The Crazy Locomotive *are logically consistent with each other. (Photo by Martha Swope.)*

co's *The Bald Soprano* a clock strikes seventeen times as the curtain rises; Mrs. Smith promptly announces that it is nine o'clock and launches into a bizarre speech on the virtues of English middle-class life. This opening quite obviously warns the audience that this play will not follow normal logic.) As any play progresses, the guidelines are revealed. The audience then expects the playwright to observe consistently the rules he has established. Even if he wishes to show that life is inconsistent or ruled by chance, the dramatist must be consistent in his depiction of inconsistency and chance. Anything that violates a play's pattern of logic (however strange that pattern would be in real life) will seem out of place and, therefore, unbelievable. It is this principle that Kenneth Burke has in mind when he declares that a work's form is created through the arousal and fulfillment of expectation.

Methods of Organizing Dramatic Action

A dramatic action is composed of incidents organized so as to accomplish some purpose. Organization is ultimately a matter of directing attention to relationships which create a meaningful pattern. The most common sources of unity are thought, character, and cause-to-effect arrangement of events.

Traditionally, the dominant organizational principle has been the *cause-to-effect* arrangement of incidents. Using this method, the playwright sets up in the opening scenes all of the necessary conditions—the situation, the desires and motivations of the characters—out of which the later events develop. The goals of one character come into conflict with those of another, or two conflicting desires within the same character may lead to a crisis. Attempts to surmount the obstacles make up the substance of the play, each scene growing logically out of those that have preceded it.

Less often, a dramatist uses a character as the principal source of unity. In this case, the incidents are held together primarily because they center around one person. Such a play may dramatize the life of a historical figure, or it may show a character's responses to a series of experiences. This kind of organization may be seen in such plays as Christopher Marlow's *Doctor Faustus* and *Tamburlaine.*

A playwright may organize his material around a *basic idea,* with the scenes linked largely because they illustrate aspects of a larger theme or argument. This type of organization is used frequently by modern playwrights, especially those of the expressionist, epic, and absurdist movements. It can be seen, for example, in Brecht's *The Private Life of the Master Race,* which treats the rise of the Nazi party in a series of scenes that illustrates the inhumanity of Nazi ideology. Many absurdist plays, such as Beckett's *Waiting for Godot,* do not develop a story so much as they embroider upon a concept, mood, or apprehension. Much drama of the 1960s resembles music in its structure since it introduces a theme and then elaborates or improvises on it. *Hair,* for example, has no throughline of action; rather it is a collection of "moments" which together seek to express the anxieties, aspirations, and ideals of youth and to declare opposition to war and to several social conventions. Instead of using linear progression to tell a clear-cut story, it tends to build spirally or vertically out of a set of motifs.

Any organizational pattern other than cause-to-effect is apt to seem loose, often giving the effect of randomness, because its incidents are not related causally. In analyzing a play, therefore, it is often essential to pinpoint the source of unity, however vague it may at first seem, for only then will it appear to be a whole rather than a collection of unrelated happenings.

Most plays from the past rely on *conflict* to arouse and maintain interest and suspense. In fact, one of the most commonly held ideas about drama is that it must involve conflict: of one character with another, of desires within the same character, of a character with his environment, of one ideology with another.

Although overt conflict plays a major role in most plays, there are dramas in which it is of little significance. Thornton Wilder's *Our Town,* for example, makes relatively little use of conflict. Instead, a narrator (the Stage Manager) begins scenes at important moments and interrupts them when his point is made. He shows a typical day in the life of a village, Grovers Corners, and suggests that morning, midday, and evening are related to childhood, maturity, and death. Although momentary conflicts occur within individual scenes, there is no major clash. Similarly, in *The Bald Soprano* events seem to occur aimlessly, and clearly they do not depend on overt conflicts.

Whether or not conflict is involved, the action of drama is usually arranged in a *climactic order*—that is, the scenes increase rather than decrease in interest. This effect is achieved through the revelation of new aspects of character or idea, by increasing suspense (the decisive moment is felt to be moving nearer and nearer), by increasing emotional intensity, or in some other way. Although the arrangement is from the lesser to the greater, within this overall movement there are moments of contrast or repose (such as the comic scenes in Shakespeare's tragedies) which afford a temporary change from the dominant pattern.

Organization may also be approached through the parts of drama, which, according to Aristotle, include *plot, character, thought, diction, music,* and *spectacle.*

Plot

Plot is often considered to be merely the summary of a play's incidents. But, though it includes the story line, it refers as well to the organization of all the elements into a meaningful pattern. Thus, plot is the overall structure of a play. In some dramas both the story and its arrangement may seem vague, but nevertheless all plays have plots, however tenuous they may be. Because the methods used in organizing plays vary widely, the most typical patterns will be emphasized here, but important deviations will be noted as well.

The Beginning. The beginning of a play usually establishes the place, the occasion, the characters, the mood, the theme, and the scheme of probability. A play is somewhat like coming upon previously unknown places and persons. Initially, the novelty may attract attention, but, as the facts about the people and the place are established, interest either wanes or increases. The playwright is faced, therefore, with a double problem:

Opening scene of King Lear *at the Oregon Shakespeare Festival, 1958. (Photo by Dwaine Smith)*

he must give essential information, but at the same time create expectations or arouse interest sufficient to make the audience desire to stay and see more.

The beginning of a play thus involves *exposition,* or the setting forth of information—about earlier events, the identity of the characters, and the present situation. While exposition is an unavoidable part of the opening scenes, it is not confined to them, for in most plays background information is only gradually revealed.

The amount of exposition required for clarity is partially determined by the *point of attack,* or the moment at which the story is taken up. Shakespeare uses an early point of attack—that is, he begins a play near the inception of the story and then tells it in clear chronological sequence. Thus, he need rely little on exposition. Greek tragedians, on the other hand, use late points of attack, which require that many prior events be summarized, and they actually show only the final parts of their stories. The amount of exposition may also depend upon the complexity of the story and its antecedents. It may vary as well according to an author's estimate of his audience. Currently, a playwright might merely refer to "Watergate" and expect his audience to supply all the necessary information surrounding it; a generation from now, however, this reference may puzzle those without considerable knowledge of history. Many playwrights in recent years have slighted exposition, probably out of the belief that audiences do not really demand that logical antecedents be supplied for everything that happens and that they are adept at picking up clues and making connections among seemingly disparate elements without having them spelled out.

Playwrights motivate exposition in various ways. For example, Ibsen most frequently introduces a character who has returned after a lengthy absence. Answers to his questions about happenings while he was away supply the needed background information. On the other hand, in a non-realistic play essential exposition may be given in a monologue. Many of Euripides' tragedies, for example, open with a prologue in which a single character summarizes past events and bemoans his present plight. In a musical, song and dance may be used for expository purposes. How exposition is used, then, depends on several factors, including: point of attack, complexity of story, scheme of probability, type of play, and the author's estimate of his audience.

In most plays from the past, attention is usually focused early on a question, potential conflict, or theme. The beginning of such plays, therefore, includes what may be called an *inciting* incident, or an occurrence that sets the main action in motion. In Sophocles' *Oedipus the King* a plague is ravishing Thebes; Oedipus has sought guidance from the oracle at Delphi, who declares that the murderer of King Laius must be found and punished before the plague can end. This is the event (introduced in the Prologue) that sets the action in motion.

The inciting incident usually leads directly to a *major dramatic question* around which the play is organized—the thread or spine that holds events together—although this question may undergo a number of changes as the play progresses. For example, the question first raised in *Oedipus the King* is: Will the murderer of Laius be found and the city saved? Later this question is modified as interest shifts to Oedipus' own guilt. Not all plays, especially recent ones, include inciting incidents or clearly identifiable major dramatic questions. Nevertheless, all have focal points, frequently a theme or controlling idea, around which the action is centered. Thus, it is always helpful to identify the unifying principle, whether it be a major dramatic question, a theme, or some other element.

The Middle. The middle of a play (at least in most of those from earlier periods) is normally composed of a series of complications. A *complication* is any new element which serves to alter the direction of the action. Complications may arise from the discovery of new information, the unexpected opposition to a plan, the necessity of choosing between courses of action, arrival of a character, introduction of a new idea, or from other sources.

Complications usually narrow the possibilities of action and create suspense. At the opening of a play the potentialities are numerous, since the story might develop in almost any direction. As characters and situation are established and as complications arise, however, the alternatives are progressively reduced. As a result, the audience comes to sense the direction of the action. As the possibilities are narrowed, a feeling of approaching crisis develops. Finally, there comes a moment when the alternatives have been so reduced that the next discovery will answer the major dramatic question. This is the moment of crisis or the peak toward which the play builds, after which there is gradual release in emotional tension leading to resolution and the play's end.

The substance of most complications is *discovery*. In one sense everything presented in a play is discovery if by that term is meant the revelation of things not previously known. The term is normally reserved, however, for occurrences of sufficient importance to alter the direction of action. Discoveries may involve objects (a wife discovers in her husband's pocket a weapon of the kind used in a murder), persons (a young man

Oedipus (Kenneth Welsh, standing center) learns the truth about his birth and parentage from an old shepherd (Oliver Cliff, kneeling) in the 1973 Guthrie Theater production of Oedipus the King designed by Desmond Heeley.

discovers that his rival in love is his brother), facts (a young man about to leave home discovers that his mother has cancer), values (a woman discovers that self-esteem is more important than marriage), or self (a man discovers that he has been acting from purely selfish motives when he thought that he was acting out of love for his children). Self-discovery is usually the most powerful.

A complication is normally introduced by one discovery and concluded by another. A complication is set in motion by the appearance of some new element which requires a new approach. But the steps taken to meet the new demands give rise to tensions and conflicts which build to a climax, or peak of intensity. The climax is accompanied, or brought about, by still another discovery which may resolve the existing complication but precipitate another. Each complication, thus, normally has a beginning, middle, and end—its own development, climax, and resolution—just as does the play as a whole.

The implications of each discovery are not always followed up immediately. Frequently a playwright is dealing with a number of characters and not every revelation involves all of them. Several complications, therefore, may intervene between the introduction of a discovery and its development. In such cases, the play pursues first one line of action and then another in an alternating or overlapping pattern.

Means other than discoveries may be used to precipitate complications. Natural disasters (such as earthquakes, storms, shipwrecks, and automobile accidents) are sometimes used. These are apt to seem especially contrived, however, if they resolve the problem (for example, if the villain is killed in an automobile accident and the struggle is automatically terminated). Frequently complications are initiated by characters acting out of ignorance. For example, a father arranges a trip for his daughter without realizing that she has fallen in love and wants to stay at home.

In most complications, the event is not as important as its effect upon the characters involved. The attempts of each to meet the situation give rise to the succeeding action and lead to new complications.

The series of complications usually culminates in the *crisis,* or turning point of the action, which opens the way for the resolution. For example, in *Oedipus the King,* Oedipus sets out to discover the murderer of Laius; the crisis comes when Oedipus realizes that he himself is the guilty person.

Not all plays have a clear-cut series of complications leading to a crisis. *Waiting for Godot,* for example, is less concerned with a progressing action than with a static condition. Nevertheless, interest is maintained by the frequent introduction of new elements: Estragon and Vladimir improvise games or plans to pass the time, and the arrival of Pozzo and Lucky creates a diversion. There is no crisis in the usual sense, only the gradual realization that man is to go on waiting, perhaps eternally.

The End. The final portion of a play, often called the *resolution* or *dénouement,* extends from the crisis to the final curtain. Although often it is brief, it may be of considerable length. It serves to tie off the various strands of action and to answer the questions raised earlier. It brings the situation back to an equilibrium and satisfies audience expectations.

The crisis normally leads to an *obligatory* scene (that is, one which the dramatist must show if the play is to be satisfying to an audience). During much of a play, important facts are hidden or ignored by the characters. The audience senses, however (either consciously or unconsciously), that eventually these facts must be revealed, since the entire action seems to point in that direction. The obligatory scene, then, answers the question: What will happen when all of the facts are revealed? It shows the opposing characters, each now with full knowledge, meeting face to face. Or it may show a single character, now recognizing his own inner conflicts and motivations, coming to grips with the implications. Since the final piece of vital information is usually withheld until the moment of crisis, the obligatory scene normally follows close upon it.

The obligatory scene may be extended over a series of complications. For example, a number of episodes may be used to show the tables being

Final scene from Friedrich Duerrenmatt's The Physicists, *as performed at Indiana University. Directed by Gary Gaiser; designed by Richard Scammon.*

turned on a man who had deceived everyone. In such cases, the resolution may be as absorbing as the complications which preceded the crisis. Normally, the resolution creates a sense of completion and fulfillment. The audience can see clearly how the ending has come about, even though it could not have predicted the outcome in advance.

Again, many plays deviate from the typical patterns. At the end of his plays, Brecht often poses questions that can only be answered outside the theatre, for he wishes to stimulate thought and action about real social conditions. Many absurdist plays are essentially circular and end much as they began so as to suggest that the events of the play will repeat themselves endlessly. This type of resolution is often found in drama organized around thought, for the ultimate purpose is to stimulate the audience to examine its own situation rather than to view the drama as a diversion from real life. Nevertheless, all plays clearly have resolutions that bring the action to a close, even if they merely imply a new beginning. Furthermore, all of a play's elements should help to create an impression that the ending is appropriate.

Character and Characterization

Character is the primary material from which plots are created, for incidents are developed mainly through the speech and behavior of dramatic personages. Characterization is the playwright's means of differentiating one dramatic personage from another. Since a dramatist may endow his creatures with few or many traits, complexity of characterization varies markedly. In analyzing roles, it is helpful to look at four levels of characterization. (This approach is adapted from a scheme suggested by Hubert Heffner in *Modern Theatre Practice* and elsewhere.)

The first level of characterization is *physical* and is concerned only with such basic facts as sex, age, size, and color. Sometimes a dramatist does not supply all of this information, but it is present whenever the play is produced, since actors necessarily give concrete form to the characters. The physical is the simplest level of characterization, however, since it reveals external traits only, many of which may not affect the dramatic action at all.

The second level is *social*. It includes a character's economic status, profession or trade, religion, family relationships—all those factors that place him in his environment.

The third level is *psychological*. It reveals a character's habitual responses, attitudes, desires, motivations, likes and dislikes—the inner workings of the mind, both emotional and intellectual, which precede action. Since habits of feeling, thought, and behavior define character more fully than do physical and social traits, and since drama most often arises from conflicting desires, the psychological is the most essential level of characterization.

The fourth level is *moral.* All plays at least imply moral concern, although they do not always emphasize it. It is most apt to be used in serious plays, especially tragedies. Although almost all human action suggests some ethical standard, in many plays the moral implications are ignored and decisions are made on grounds of expediency. This is typical of comedy, since moral deliberations tend to make any action serious. More significantly than any other kind, moral decisions differentiate characters, since the choices they make when faced with moral crises show whether they are selfish, hypocritical, honest, or whatever. A moral decision usually causes a character to examine his own motives and values, in the process of which his true nature is revealed both to himself and to the audience.

A playwright may emphasize one or more of these levels. Some writers pay little attention to the physical appearance of their characters, concentrating instead upon psychological and moral traits; other dramatists may describe appearance and social status in detail. In assessing the completeness of a characterization, however, it is not enough merely to make a list of traits and levels of characterization. It is also necessary to ask *how the character functions in the play.* For example, the audience needs to know little about the maid who only appears to announce dinner; any detailed characterization would be superfluous and distracting. On the other hand, the principal characters usually need to be drawn in greater depth. The appropriateness and completeness of each characterization, therefore, may be judged only after analyzing its function in each scene and in the play as a whole.

A character is revealed in several ways: through *descriptions in stage directions, prefaces,* or *other explanatory material* not part of the dialogue or action; through *what the character says*; through *what others say about him*; and, perhaps most important, through *what he does*. It is not enough, however, for a dramatist to assign characteristics to his personages; some action must be motivated, or some idea clarified, by each quality if it is not to be irrelevant or even misleading. The relative importance of each trait, therefore, must be assessed in terms of its function in the play.

It is not always easy to perceive a character's true nature, since information about him is usually given in fragments scattered throughout the play. Furthermore, many different or even contradictory images of him may be presented. For example, a character may see himself as a certain kind of person; for one reason or another, however, he may try to project a different image to others; in turn, each of the other characters will see him from a different angle. Because the dramatist builds character through this composite approach, the audience must always watch for clues that indicate which statements and actions are to be accepted as accurate revelations of character. Sometimes, however, as in Harold Pinter's plays, it is virtually impossible to resolve the ambiguities, and, in fact, the uncertainty may be an important ingredient in the playwright's outlook and method.

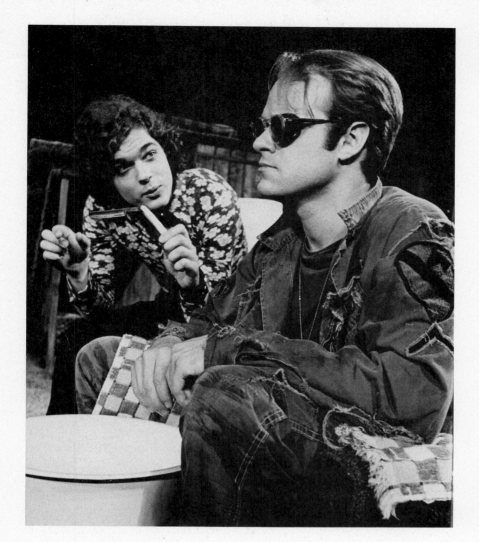

*Alan Cauldwell (left) as Rick
and Drew Snyder as David in a
climactic moment of Rabe's*
Sticks and Bones. *(Photo by
Friedman-Abeles.)*

Characters are defined in much the same way as are words: First they
are placed in a broad category (typified), and then differentiated (individualized) from other examples of the same type. *Typification* is necessary
if characters are to be placed in the context of human experience. If a
character were totally unlike any person the spectators had ever known,
they would be unable to understand him. Most characters may be placed
in a category, such as the doting mother, the bashful young man, or the
ambitious executive. But if the playwright goes no further, the audience
will probably find the personages oversimplified and will see them as
"type" characters. Therefore, most dramatists assign several traits which
serve to *individualize* characers within the broad categories. Thus, typify-
ing qualities make a character recognizable and familiar, while indivi-
dualizing traits make him unusual and complex.

A playwright may be concerned with making his characters *sympathetic* or *unsympathetic*. Most frequently, sympathetic characters are created by assigning traits admired in real life, but many modern playwrights have created sympathy for anormative characters by exploring the reasons behind behavior, showing characters as rebels against a hypocritical society or as victims of circumstances more worthy of compassion than vilification. Normally, however, sympathetic characters are given major virtues and lesser foibles, while the reverse procedure is used for unsympathetic characters. The more a character is made either completely good or bad, the more he is apt to become unacceptable as a truthful reflection of human behavior.

Acceptability, however, is in part determined by the type of play or the scheme of probability. Melodrama, for example, oversimplifies human psychology and clearly divides characters and actions into good and evil. Tragedy, on the other hand, normally depicts more complex forces at work both within and without man, and requires greater depth of characterization than does melodrama, which may function very well with type characters. The audience usually expects only that characterization be appropriate to the play's action and thought.

Thought

The third basic element of a play is *thought*. It includes the themes, the arguments, the overall meaning, focus, or significance of the action. It is present in all plays, even those that seem to be without purpose, for a playwright cannot avoid expressing ideas through the events and characterizations of the play, which always imply some view of human behavior. Thought is also one of the major sources of unity in drama, for action may be organized around a central idea, motif, or concern. This kind of unity is typical of much recent drama.

In thought, a play is both general and specific. For example, *King Lear* dramatizes in part the general topic of child–parent relationships, but it does so through the complex story of intrigues among the ruling class in England's legendary past. Thus, the general topic, or theme, serves as a point of focus around which events cluster, while the specific story gives concreteness to ideas which otherwise would be too abstract. Although a play may have a number of themes, one is usually dominant. One key to a play, therefore, lies in its thought. By identifying the major motifs and examining how they have been embodied we can recognize the author's over-all purpose and methods.

The general and specific subjects of a play are related to the concepts of universality and individuality. *Universality* is the quality that enables a play to communicate with audiences, even though centuries may have passed since it was written. To say that *Hamlet* has universal significance does not mean that we should be able to put ourselves in Hamlet's position as a prince or as the avenger of his father's death. The universal elements are to be found in the conflict between a son's duty to his father and his feelings for his mother, between personal integrity and religious faith, between justice and corrupt political power, and between the "underdog" and overwhelming forces. These are situations that might confront human beings of any social class in any period. They provide points of contact between Hamlet and the audience.

On the other hand, every story must be *individualized* if it is to be believable and interesting. *Hamlet,* therefore, has many elements that depart markedly from normal experience and keep the story from being hackneyed and overly familiar. However, some modern dramatists, such as Wilder and Ionesco, have reversed the normal process. They have chosen the most commonplace events, but have treated them in such a way as to make them seem strange. Thus, they force the audience to view the familiar in a new light.

The significance, or "meaning," of a play is normally implied rather than directly stated. It is to be discovered in the relationships among characters, the ideas associated with sympathetic and unsympathetic characters, the conflicts and their resolutions, the spectacle, and such devices as music and song. Sometimes, however, the author's intention is clearly stated in the script. The characters may advocate a certain line of action, point of view, or specific social reform. Dramas using such methods used to be called *propaganda* or *social problem* plays because of their aim to persuade an audience to act or think in a particular way. Although these terms are no longer in wide use, the type of play they describe has continued to be popular, perhaps most notably with radical theatre groups of the late 1960s.

An author wishing to persuade an audience has two paths open to him. He may subordinate his message and depend upon the implications to be sufficiently persuasive. In this case, he risks being misunderstood. Or, he may make his position quite clear (usually through a direct statement by an admirable character or by oversimplifying the issues to make the choices clear). In this case, while the dramatist leaves no doubt as to his purpose, he may alienate his audience, who may conclude that the play has been an excuse for delivering a sermon or social message. In the hands of the unskillful dramatist such sermonizing is frequently the result. Expert dramatists, however, like Ibsen and Shaw, have made themselves relatively clear while creating compelling and vital plays.

The dramatist who is intent upon achieving *complete* clarity must restrict the meanings of words and actions and in doing so may eliminate those connotations and implications which suggest that the significance of the drama extends far beyond the immediate story. Yet ambiguity is basic to human experience: Life does not come equipped with meanings which are unmistakable; we ponder over our experience and try to find significance in it, but we can never be certain that we have solved the riddles. Since human experience is the raw material of drama, the playwright who sees no ambiguities in life may well create a world on the stage which is too simple for an audience to accept. On the other hand, everyone simplifies experience in the process of seeking its significance. Since the dramatist is usually concerned with the patterns behind the infinite detail of life, he must eliminate what he considers irrelevant. His selection, nevertheless, must command belief.

Dramatists in different periods have used various devices to project ideas. Greek playwrights made extensive use of the *chorus,* just as those of later periods employed such devices as *soliloquies, asides,* and other forms of *direct statement.* Still other tools for projecting meaning are *allegory* and *symbol.* In allegory, characters are often personifications (good deeds, mercy, greed, and so on), and the meaning of the play can usually be reduced to a clear moral statement. Its use can be seen most clearly in a play such as *Everyman.* A symbol is a concrete object or event which, while meaningful in itself, also suggests a concept or set of relationships. For example, the orchard in Chekhov's *The Cherry Orchard* is both a real object and a symbol. As an object, once useful, then admired merely for its beauty, it is finally destroyed to make way for homes that will be occupied by merchants. As a symbol, it represents the Russian aristocracy, which, having lost its usefulness, must make way for the more vigorous middle class. The orchard takes on a double meaning—literal and symbolic—enabling it to comment not only on the characters in the play but also on Russian society in general. The symbol has been a favorite device with modern writers, for it allows them to suggest deeper meanings even within a realistic framework. Contemporary dramatists have made considerable use of such devices as songs and projections to convey or induce thought. Thus, although approaches vary widely, all plays comment on human experience in some way.

Diction

Plot, character, and thought are the basic ingredients of drama; to convey these to an audience, the playwright has at his disposal only two means—sound and spectacle—since the spectator takes in a theatrical experience almost wholly through the ear and the eye. Sound includes language, music, and other aural effects; spectacle includes all the visual elements of a production (physical movement and dance, costumes, scenery, properties, and lighting).

Although it has been fashionable in recent years to denigrate the importance of words in the theatre, language is still the playwright's primary means of expression. When a play is performed, other expressive means (primarily music and spectacle) may be added, but to convey his conceptions to others, the dramatist depends almost entirely on dialogue and stage directions. Thus, language (or diction) is the dramatist's most essential tool.

Diction serves many purposes. First, it is used to *impart information*. Through it, the playwright sets forth the essential facts, ideas, and emotional responses of characters in each scene.

Second, diction is used to *characterize*. It is from his speeches that we perceive the emotion and intellectual motivations and responses of each character in a play.

Third, language is used to *direct attention* to important plot elements. Since significant information and responses must be emphasized, dialogue points up conflicts and complications and prepares for further developments. It builds suspense by making the audience aware of potential outcomes, for while scenes always occur in the present, they constantly direct attention toward possible future results and create a sense of forward movement and expectancy.

Fourth, diction is used to *reveal the themes and ideas* of a play. It provides clues to significant meanings while it is revealing character and developing action.

Fifth, language helps to *establish tone and scheme of probability*. It indicates whether the play is comic or serious, farcical or tragic. It also suggests the degree of abstration from reality. Sometimes the use of poetry indicates that the play will not follow ordinary causality. The choice of words, the number of colloquialisms, the length of lines, and other linguistic devices are clues to the scheme of probability within which the play is operating.

Characterization occurs on several levels. In Sticks and Bones, *produced by Joseph Papp in 1971, the bodily postures, facial expressions, and costumes give the audience many insights into the characters.*

Sixth, diction helps to *establish tempo and rhythm*. Tempo is the pace at which a scene is played. The tempo of a love scene is apt to be much more leisurely than that of a dueling scene, for example, and the diction usually reflects and helps to create the proper tempo. Rhythm is the recurring pattern which results from the flow of speeches. Halting speech gives rise to one rhythmical pattern, and animated, excited speech to another. Tempo and rhythm together create a sense of forward movement or of retarded action. When the rhythm of each scene is built to a climax (much like a movement in a symphony), it helps to hold attention and arouse expectancy.

The diction of every play, no matter how realistic, is more abstract and formal than that of normal conversation. A dramatist always selects, arranges, and heightens language more than anyone ever does in spontaneous speech. Consequently, in a realistic play, although the dialogue is modeled after everyday usage, the characters are more articulate and state their ideas and feelings more precisely than their real-life counterparts do. On the other hand, realistic dialogue may retain the rhythms, tempos, and basic vocabulary of colloquial speech.

The dialogue of nonrealistic plays may deviate markedly from normal speech. Sometimes, everyday patterns are reduced to a mere skeleton, as in expressionistic drama, the dialogue of which is sometimes labeled "telegraphic" because every superfluous word has been eliminated. At other times, the clichés of ordinary conversation are emphasized until they become ludicrous, as in many of Ionesco's plays. More frequently, however, nonrealistic drama employs a larger vocabulary, abandons the rhythms of conversation, and makes considerable use of imagery and meter. A larger vocabulary allows a more precise choice of words, avoids the repetitiveness typical of colloquial speech, and permits more forceful expression when characters must transcend the ordinary.

Imagery is always found in poetic drama, but it may appear in realistic prose plays as well. The simile is widely used even in everyday speech ("He was as mad as a hornet," or "She's as nervous as a cat on a hot tin roof"). A simile makes a direct comparison between two qualities or things and helps to point up likenesses which reveal character, situation, or meaning. A metaphor makes an indirect comparison between dissimilarities ("God is my fortress"). There are many other kinds of imagery, but all point to comparisons, connotations, or implications which enlarge or alter the literal meaning. Furthermore, the use of a large number of similar images affects the tone of a play. The dark, somber quality of *Hamlet,* for example, is partially explained by the overwhelming number of images in it concerned with death and decay. Although an audience may not be aware of images, it is unconsciously influenced by them.

Diction, like the other elements of a play, uses both the familiar and the unfamiliar, the typical and the individual. Aristotle states that good dialogue should be both *clear* and *distinctive.* He goes on to explain that clarity depends upon the use of ordinary words, but warns that familiar words used alone may lead to dullness. He observes, "Diction becomes distinguished and nonprosaic by the use of unfamiliar terms, i.e., strange words, metaphors, lengthened forms, and everything that deviates from the ordinary modes of speech. But a whole statement in such terms will be either a riddle or a barbarism." Good diction, then, usually strikes a middle ground between overly familiar and overly strange language. The familiar gives clarity, the strange or unusual adds variety.

Diction should also be *adapted to the stage*. Sometimes a dramatist writes speeches which sound stilted and unnatural when spoken because he has failed to take into account both the possibilities and the limitations of the voice and ear. The good playwright is concerned with how dialogue will sound, and how the human voice will affect the written word.

The basic criterion for judging diction, however, is its *appropriateness* to the characters, the situation, the scheme of probability, and the type of play. Almost any dialouge will be acceptable to an audience if it is in keeping with the other elements in the script.

Music

Music, as ordinarily understood, is not a part of every play. But, if the term is extended to include all patterned sound, it may be considered an important ingredient in every production. In this expanded sense, music includes all sound effects, the actors' voices, songs, and instrumental music.

In the preceding section, language was described as the playwright's primary means of expression. But a written script (like a musical score) is not fully activated until the performers—through the elements of pitch, stress, volume, tempo, duration, and quality—transform print into sound. It is also through the manipulation of these elements that meaning is conveyed. Although the words of a speech may remain constant, their implications can be varied considerably by altering one or more of the elements. For example, note the numerous shades of meaning that may be imparted to so simple a speech as "You say he told her" by shifting the emphasis from one word to another, or by altering the tone from anger to sarcasm to questioning or wonder. A playwright may know precisely what he wishes to convey in speech, but a director or actor may not perceive this intent, and therefore may give the speech a quite different interpretation. A dramatist cannot guard against all misinterpretations, but he can lessen them if he writes for the voice and ear as well as for the eye.

Dialogue varies considerably in its formal qualities. In some plays, it simulates the loosely controlled rhythms of everyday speech, but in others, such as in Shakespearean drama, it is shaped into a highly formalized pattern. In delivery, the effective actor respects the pattern, for it is one of the devices used by the playwright to define characters and their world. It is not always easy, however, to accept or render patterns that deviate from

Cast members at the climax of a production number in A Little Night Music. *(Photo by Martha Swope.)*

normal speech. For example, it is often said that contemporary American actors have lost the art of speaking Shakespearean verse and that they convert it into prose.

Song formalizes speech even more than does verse. A musical setting usually supplies rather precise directions as to how the words are to be rendered: the key signature and the melody specify at what pitch each syllable is to be uttered, and the notation prescribes the duration of each sound; directions for tempo and volume are also normally given by the composer; and the combination of elements determines the over all mood or tonal quality. Thus, the writer of songs goes much beyond the writer of dialogue in specifying the pattern of sound to be heard in performance. The actor is permitted considerably more discretion in vocal delivery than is the singer, although some musical compositions allow the singer room for vocal embellishments and similar personal touches.

Instrumental music may accompany lyrics or be used to underscore dialogue, but it may dispense with words altogether. It may be played by a single instrument or many. Since each instrument has distinctive tonal characteristics, the mood and texture of instrumental music may be varied almost endlessly by using a solo instrument or by varying the types and numbers of instruments in combination.

A play, then, may use no formal music, may introduce one or more incidental songs, or may utilize (as in musical comedy and opera) song and instrumental accompaniment as integral structural means.

Music serves many functions. First, it can *establish or enhance mood and create expectations*. The overture to a musical (or the incidental music used to precede scenes in a nonmusical drama) usually reflects the tone of what is to follow and thereby increases the audience's receptivity. In the nineteenth century, music was used regularly (as it now is in movies) to underscore and build the emotional qualities of scenes. While contemporary playwrights usually avoid the obvious sentimentality of early melodrama, many nevertheless rely heavily on music to create mood and tone.

Second, music can help to *establish the scheme of probability*. The liberal use of music is normally an indication that the playwright is departing markedly from the patterns of everyday life and that the audience should not expect the incidents to be entirely realistic. On the other hand, music may be used extensively in realistic drama, provided its inclusion is logically explained.

Third, music can *characterize*. Melody, rhythm, and tempo (in combination with lyrics) can establish the traits of a dramatic character, often in a single song.

Fourth, music can be a *medium for ideas*. Brecht often uses songs to raise questions or to reflect on events. He often deliberately uses musical settings at variance in tone with the lyrics in order to create conflict in the mind of the audience about the song's intent. Somewhat similarly, many contemporary playwrights have used song as a medium for protest, questioning, or agitation.

Fifth, music can *condense*. It can speed up characterization, and provide exposition quickly (as is typical of the opening scenes of musical comedy). It may also be used to telescope processes which otherwise occur over a long period of time. (For example, in *My Fair Lady*, the transformation of Liza Doolittle's speech patterns is shown primarily through a single musical number, "The Rain in Spain.") Furthermore, if early in the play the composer relates certain melodies or musical motifs to specific events or characters, the mere playing of a melodic phrase later will remind the audience of earlier occurrences.

Sixth, music can *lend variety*. Not only can music itself be endlessly varied, it can provide far greater variety to a play than is possible with the spoken word alone.

Seventh, music can be *pleasurable in itself*, for it is enjoyable quite apart from its dramatic uses.

As with spectacle, music is not always clearly specified in a script. In fact, except in the case of operas and musical comedies, a musical score seldom accompanies the printed text. Even then, unless one has the training to read music and the ability mentally to translate a score into sound, it is difficult to apprehend how music will alter the effect gained from a reading of the play. Therefore, in analyzing scripts, criticis usually ignore the musical element, although when they write about the same plays in performance, they may say much about it.

Spectacle

After sound, the visual elements of a play are the dramatist's principal means of expression. But, since he normally depends upon others to supply these elements when the play is produced, the author does not have full control over them. In recent years, as the importance of language has been challenged, the visual element has often dominated the aural. Because the playwright seldom describes spectacle precisely, other theatre artists, even when they wish to be entirely faithful to his intentions, must base their work on deductions gained from analyzing plot, characterization, thought, and dialogue.

The functions of spectacle are several. First, spectacle *gives information*. It helps to establish where and when the action occurs (a living room, a castle, a prison, or a composite of many places; the historical period, the time of day, the country), or it may indicate that time and place are irrelevant.

Second, spectacle *aids characterization*. It helps to establish such social factors as the economic level, the class, and the profession to which the characters belong. It aids in projecting the psychological aspects of character by demonstrating tastes (in the clothes worn, the rooms in which the characters live, and the like). Psychological factors are also revealed through the spatial relationships among characters (not always apparent in a script but always seen in a production).

Third, spectacle helps to *establish the scheme of probability*. An abstract setting suggests one scheme, while a completely realistic setting may indicate another. Costumes, lighting, the actors' gestures and movement all establish the play's context of reality.

Fourth, spectacle *establishes mood and atmosphere* by giving clues about the relative seriousness of the action, and by providing the proper environment in relation to a play's form and style.

Spectacle, like the other elements of a play, should be *appropriate, expressive of the play's values, distinctive, and practicable*. (The problems of transferring the written script to the stage are treated at length in Part 3 of this book.)

Form in Drama

These six parts—plot, character, thought, diction, music, and spectacle—make up every play. But they may be combined and varied in ways almost infinitely. Nevertheless, certain basic patterns have recurred sufficiently often to permit us to divide plays into a limited number of dramatic forms. Because as a term it has been used to designate a variety of concepts, *form* is difficult to define. Basically, however, it means the arrangement (or overall pattern) of a work of art.

Charles Kean's production of Shakespeare's Henry VIII *in 1859. The scenery and costumes typify the antiquarian approach in vogue at that time. (Courtesy of the Victoria and Albert Museum. Crown Copyright.)*

There are three principal determinants of form. First, form is affected by the material being shaped. In actuality, it is difficult, if not impossible, to separate form and matter, since no one can comprehend a formless object or idea. Nevertheless, the matter (the action, characters, mood, and thought) of comedy differs sufficiently from that of tragedy to indicate that one has been shaped to arouse laughter or ridicule while the other is designed to create pity or fear.

Second, the writer (or the maker of an artistic object) is a determinant of form. Each man's view of life and art differs somewhat from that of others, and his own peculiar talents and intentions show in his work. Thus, while both Sophocles and Euripides wrote tragedies, the forms of their plays show certain differences. Third, the intended purpose of an object helps to determine its form. Just as a chair's shape differs from that of a desk because it is created to fulfill a different need, so the design of a tragedy differs from that of a comedy.

Since no two plays ever have the same material, author, and purpose, each play is unique. On the other hand, plays share many qualities. Because each play is both unique and similar to other works, two major approaches to form have developed: one treats form as *fixed* and the other as *organic*. The doctrine of *fixed forms* rests upon the belief that the characteristics of dramatic types can be clearly isolated and defined. This was the usual position from the Renaissance until about 1750. Many adherents of this view have also suggested that a play may be judged according to how well it fulfills the requirements of its particular type. The doctrine of *organic form,* on the other hand, is based on the belief that a play takes shape and grows as a plant does, and that each play must be free to follow its own needs and laws without reference to any preexisting ideas about form.

Each of these two views is partially defensible. Most plays can be classified according to type, and the major characteristics of each type can be listed. Furthermore, in criticizing a play, it is usually helpful to compare it with other works of similar type; using categories as points of reference can also save much time (for example, a term such as *comedy of manners* summarizes many qualities and communicates quickly, provided that a reader understands the meaning of the designation).

On the other hand, each play is unique in some respects and should be appreciated for its individuality. Often it is impossible to classify a play according to form, and the attempt to label it may assume more importance than understanding it. For example, arguments as to whether *Death of a Salesman* can rightfully be called a tragedy have frequently consumed undue attention in discussions. One form is not necessarily better than another, for there are both excellent and poor examples of each form. Furthermore, a play is not necessarily defective because it does not fit some abstract idea of form. For example, our inability to categorize *Waiting for Godot* neatly does not lessen that play's effectiveness. Thus, while the classification of plays according to form may be helpful, it can also be misused.

An almost endless number of forms and subforms have been suggested by critics. Since it would be impossible to define all of the labels that have been used, the basic forms will be discussed and then deviations will be noted. All labels used to describe dramatic forms can be related to one of three basic qualities: the serious, the comic, and the seriocomic. In turn, these three divisions are epitomized in three forms: tragedy, comedy, and melodrama.

Tragedy. A tragedy presents a genuinely serious action and maintains a mood throughout that underscores the play's serious intention (although there may be moments of comic relief). It raises important questions about the meaning of man's existence, his moral nature, and his social or psychological relationships.

Most tragedies written prior to the eighteentth century show the interaction between cosmic and human forces: a god, providence, or some moral power independent of man usually affects the outcome of the action almost as much as do the human agents. Many tragedies imply that the protagonist has violated a moral order which must be vindicated and reestablished. Because superhuman forces are involved, the outcome often seems inevitable and predetermined.

In the eighteenth century, the supernatural element began to decline as social and psychological forces were given increased emphasis and as the conflicts were gradually reduced to strictly human ones. Eventually the action no longer involved man's will in conflict with divine laws, but was restricted to conflict among human desires, laws, and institutions. Since strictly human problems may be more readily understood and solved, happy resolutions were more probable. Because this later drama has often been concerned with everyday situations and seems less profound than earlier works, many criticis have refused to call it tragedy and have substituted the term *drama* or *drame*.

The protagonist of tragedy is usually a person who arouses our sympathy and admiration —which in some cases, however, may be limited. Macbeth, Richard III, and Medea, for example, are tragic protagonists who have noble qualities and whose indomitable wills we can admire, but whose actions we cannot condone. Normally, the protagonist is ethically superior without being perfect: he is sufficiently above the average to inspire admiration, but is sufficiently imperfect to be believably human and at least partially responsible for his own downfall.

Most often, the tragic protagonist encounters disaster through his pursuit of a worthy aim, but, on following one ideal, he violates some other moral or social law which overpowers him. A recurring motif of serious drama is the imposition of a duty, the performance of which will inevita-

David Garrick in the storm scene of King Lear. *Note the eighteenth-century garments. From a contemporary engraving after a painting by Wilson. (Courtesy University of Iowa Library.)*

bly lead to loss of life, love, reputation, or peace of mind. The protagonist (Hamlet, for example) is faced therefore with choosing between two goals, each of which under other circumstances would be good, but which have been placed in seemingly irreconcilable opposition. Another recurring motif in tragedy (seen in *Oedipus the King* and *King Lear*) is man's inability to control his destiny.

In most tragedies written prior to the eighteenth century the protagonists are members of the ruling class, but in succeeding periods they have been drawn increasingly from the middle or lower classes. Many critics have questioned whether the average man can acquire the stature necessary to a tragic hero. There seems little basis, however, for the assumption that social class has any connection with nobility of character and action. Although most modern serious drama is less powerful than the best tragedies of the Greek and Elizabethans, the difference is one of degree and is probably related to man's reduced estimate of his place in the whole scheme of being. (The reverence accorded to tragedy seldom extends to other forms; for example, few critics have even implied that a play should not be called a comedy merely because it is less powerful than certain other comedies or because it differs from the work of other periods.)

The emotional effect of tragedy is usually described as the "arousal of pity and fear," but these basic emotions include a wide range of other responses: understanding, compassion, admiration, apprehension, foreboding, dread, awe, and terror. Pity and fear are rooted in two instinctive human reactions: fear in the desire for self-preservation and pity in concern for the welfare of others. Aristotle, in the *Poetics,* states that pity is aroused by the apprehension of some pain or harm about to befall someone like ourselves, and that were we in the position of the endangered person we would feel fear. Thus, pity and fear are complementary emotions. To feel pity, we must perceive some likeness between ourselves and the tragic character, and we must be able to imagine ourselves in his situation. Aristotle further argues that if we fear too much for ourselves we cannot pity others, for panic drives out altruistic concerns. Fear, then, is an emotion which stems from the instinct for self-preservation, while pity transcends self-concern. Fear enables us to empathize with the struggling protagonist, while pity carries us outside ourselves and unites us with man's struggle for integrity. The degree to which these responses are aroused by a particular play depends upon the nature of the protagonist and the action, and upon the capacity of the spectator to experience these emotions.

In addition to arousing pity and fear, tragedy also calms or purges these emotions. Rather than leaving us emotionally unsettled, the ending of a tragedy releases the tensions that have been aroused and brings us back to a state of equilibrium. It not only resolves the situation which has aroused pity and fear but it also leads us to recognize the inevitability of the outcome and to perceive its implications.

Comedy. The action of comedy is based on some deviation from nor-

Scene from Tartuffe *as directed by Roger Planchon, one of the most respected of contemporary French producers. (Photo by Pic.)*

mality in action, character, thought, or speech. The deviation, however, must not pose a serious threat to the well-being of the normal, and a comic (or "in fun") mood must be maintained. There is no subject, however trivial or important, that cannot be treated in comedy provided it is placed in a framework which exploits its incongruities.

Comedy also demands that the audience view situation, characters, or ideas objectively. Henri Bergson, in *Laughter,* has stated that comedy requires "an anesthesia of the heart," for it is difficult to laugh at anything with which we are too closely allied either through sympathy or dislike. For example, we might find the sight of a man slipping on a banana peel ludicrous, but if we discover that he has recently undergone a serious operation, our concern will destroy the laughter. Likewise, we may dislike some things so intensely that we cannot see their ridiculous qualities. On the other hand, an audience is not objective about all elements of a comedy, for sympathy is aroused for the norm. Part of comic pleasure comes from witnessing the eventual triumph of normative behavior, characters or ideas over a threat from the abnormal.

Because of its wide range, comedy is often divided into a number of subcategories. All the classifications, however, can be related to three variables: the extent to which the action focuses on situation, character, or thought; the degree of objectivity with which the protagonist is treated; and the nature and implications of the action. Consequently, the three basic types are comedies of situation, comedies of character, and comedies of idea, although each may be further divided into one or more subtypes.

A *comedy of situation* shows the ludicrous results of placing characters in unusual circumstances. For example, a number of persons are planning to attend a masked ball, but each, for his own reasons, tries to conceal his intentions. The devices for getting rid of each other, the attempts to elude discovery when all appear at the ball, the reactions upon being recognized, and the eventual reconciliation of the characters make up the comic action. In such a play, character and idea are of minor importance.

Many critics treat *farce* as a separate form, although there is little to distinguish it from a comedy of situation. Farce is often used as a classification for those plays, or portions of plays, which rely principally upon buffoonery, accident, and coincidence. Pies in the face, beatings, the naïve or mistaken views of characters, the ludicrous situation arising from coincidence or circumstantial evidence exemplify the devices of farce. Often it seems a kind of inspired nonsense with situations so obviously contrived that a sensible word from any character would resolve the action at once. Farce is sometimes said to have no purpose beyond entertainment. While it is true that most farces seem devoid of serious purpose, elements of farce have been important ingredients in many of the world's finest comedies, including those of Aristophanes and Molière.

A *comedy of character* grows out of the eccentricities of the protagonist. For example, some of Molière's best plays are built around characters suffering from hypochondria, miserliness, or hypocrisy.

Although it may draw some of its characteristics from comedies of situation or idea, *romantic comedy* is most closely related to the comedy of character, for it usually treats the struggles—often those centering around a love affair—of characters who are basically admirable. It is best illustrated by Shakespeare's *Twelfth Night* and *As You Like It,* in which the main characters are lovers pursuing normal and sympathetic goals. A comic response is aroused primarily because of the ludicrous devices the characters use in pursuing success and the misunderstandings or complication that result. In romantic comedy the more boisterous action is usually relegated to subplots involving minor but ridiculous characters. Thus, it reverses the pattern found in a comedy of character.

A *comedy of ideas* has as its principal focus a conflict over a concept or a way of thought. It is probably best exemplified in the work of George Bernard Shaw and Aristophanes.

While the *comedy of manners* shares some traits with the comedy of situation and of character, it is most nearly related to the comedy of ideas, for it exploits the incongruities that arise from adherence to an accepted code of behavior at the expense of normal desires and responses. As a label, comedy of manners is sometimes reserved for plays about aristocratic and sophisticated characters who indulge in sparkling and witty repartee, attributes that have also given currency to an alternative label, *comedy of wit.*

Social comedy is still another variation on the comedy of ideas, for it explores social values, standards of behavior, or accepted ways of thought. If it aims at remedying society or behavior, it may be called *corrective comedy*.

Although most comedies can be placed in one of the categories just listed, almost all have elements that relate them to several types. A comedy of character, for instance, may use devices normally associated with farce, a comedy of manners, or a comedy of ideas. Labels, therefore, need to be used with some flexibility if they are to be helpful.

All comedy seeks to arouse emotions which lie in a range between joy and scorn. At one extreme, Shakespeare's romantic comedies elicit a response that can best be described as a feeling of well-being. They may arouse smiles or quiet laughter but seldom boisterous laughter. At the other extreme, Ben Jonson's *Volpone* at times becomes almost too painful for laughter. These extremes of the gentlest teasing and the bitterest ridicule mark the limits of comic response.

Comedy seldom (except through implication) raises great moral questions, as does tragedy. Rather, it concentrates on man in his social relationships. It reaffirms the need for a society that allows normal human impulses adequate scope while putting a check on deviations that threaten to destroy what is valuable in it. As conceptions about normative behavior vary from one era to another, the scope of comedy changes accordingly.

Melodrama. Although the term *melodrama* was not widely used until the nineteenth century, the type had existed since the fifth century B.C. In some periods it has been called *tragicomedy,* and today it is often labeled *drama* because the term *melodrama* is in disrepute.

A melodrama deals with a serious action. Its seriousness, however, is only temporary and is usually attributable to the malicious designs of an unsympathetic character. A happy resolution is achieved, therefore, by neutralizing or destroying the power of the villain.

Since melodrama depicts a world in which good and evil are clearly separated, the conflict almost always involves a sharply defined moral code. There is seldom any question as to where the audience's sympathy should lie.

The characters in melodrama are usually divided into those who are almost completely sympathetic and those who are almost completely antipathetic. For the sake of variety, there may also be one or more simpleminded or uninhibited characters who provide comic relief. The unsympathetic characters usually set in motion the complications, while the sympathetic characters seek only to deal with the danger. Thus, the characters do not grow and change, as in tragedy, for the moral nature of each is established at the beginning of the play and remains constant throughout.

The action of melodrama usually develops a powerful threat against the well-being of an admirable and innocent protagonist. It shows his entanglement in a web of circumstances and his eventual rescue from death or

Many variations on melodrama were exploited in the nineteenth century. Among the most popular was equestrian drama, which combined daring horsemanship with melodramatic plots. The illustration above depicts a performance at Astley's Amphitheatre in London in 1815. (From Londina Illustrata.)

ruin, usually at the last possible moment. (Most contemporary television series dealing with crime and danger are melodramas.)

The appeals of melodrama are strong and basic, since the incidents, which seek to build the most intense suspense, create a desire to see wronged innocence vindicated and unchecked evil chastised. The emotions aroused by melodrama range from dread and concern for the protagonist to hatred for the antagonist.

Melodrama has a double ending in which the good characters are rescued and rewarded and the evil are detected and punished. Thus, it is related to tragedy through the seriousness of its action and to comedy through its happy conclusion. It has been a popular form throughout history, for it assures audiences that good triumphs over evil.

Mixed Forms. Although tragedy, comedy, and melodrama are the primary forms, many plays do not fit comfortably into any of these three categories. For example, some works, although basically serious, do not achieve "the sense of high purpose" which we associate with tragedy; thus, we may seek other labels to set them off from plays which are more clearly tragic. Other dramas shift tone frequently from comic to serious and may end either happily or unhappily; consequently, it may be difficult to decide whether they are more nearly comedies or tragedies. Still other works have all the marks of melodrama until the end, when the failure to reward the good and punish the evil characters raises questions about the play's type.

This mixing of characteristics is probably most typical of modern times, when playwrights have often deliberately departed from the traditional forms. For example, Ionesco has labeled some of his works "anti-plays" or "tragic farces," while Harold Pinter called his early plays "comedies of menace," and Michel de Ghelderode subtitled some of his works "burlesque mysteries" and "tragedies of the music hall." Although these designations indicate significant departures from the conventional forms, most also suggest a connection with them. For example, Ionesco's use of "tragic farce" to describe *The Chairs* indicates his awareness of manipulating comic techniques to make an audience perceive the seriousness behind the semifarcical events. Similarly, his use of "anti-play" to describe *The Bald Soprano* shows his deliberate departure from traditional structural patterns, although, as in *The Chairs,* the dramatic devices are essentially those of comedy.

In reading plays that deviate from the traditional forms, it is probably of little help to insist upon clear-cut type designations. On the other hand, it may be illuminating to note in each the tendencies toward tragedy, comedy, or melodrama, since this may clarify the ways and the extent to which comic, serious, and seriocomic elements have been mingled. Nevertheless, the fact that so much modern drama does not fit into the traditional categories demonstrates the danger of overemphasizing formal classifications. Identifying a play's type is important only because it may help to define its purpose and because it provides a basis for comparing it with other works having similar characteristics. Classification is only one step toward understanding a play and is no substitute for careful analysis.

Style

When we categorize plays, we should recognize that even plays of the same type vary considerably. One cause of this variety is style. Like form, style is difficult to define because it has been used to designate many concepts. Basically, however, *style* is a quality which results from a characteristic mode of expression or method of presentation.

Style may stem from traits attributable to a period, a nation, a movement, or an author. In most periods, the drama of all Western nations has certain common qualities that may be attributed to the prevailing religious, philosophical, and psychological concepts and to current dramatic and theatrical conventions. Thus, we may speak of an eighteenth-century style. Within a period, however, there are national differences that permit us to distinguish a French from an English style. Furthermore, the dramas written by neoclassicists demonstrate qualities that permit us to identify the stylistic features of that movement and to distinguish them from those written by romantics, expressionists, or absurdists. Finally, the plays of individual authors have distinctive qualities that set them off from the work of all other writers. Thus, we may speak of Shakespeare's or of Sophocles' style.

Most discussions of style in theatre and drama consider only period and artistic movement. Style is usually divided into such categories as classicism, neoclassicism, romanticism, realism, naturalism, expressionism, symbolism, absurdism, epic theatre, and so on. Since each category is associated with specific periods, it is usually discussed in connection with style as it relates to an age. (The chronological survey of theatre and drama in

Scene from US, *a documentary play conceived and directed by Peter Brook with the Royal Shakespeare Company. (Courtesy Royal Shakespeare Company.)*

Part 2 will treat style more fully as it applies to periods and movements.)

Style in drama results from two basic influences. First, it is grounded upon assumptions about truth and reality. Dramatists of different movements or periods have all sought to convey truthful pictures of the human predicament, but they have differed widely in their answers to these fundamental questions: What constitutes ultimate truth? By what process can we perceive reality? At times it has been argued that surface appearances merely disguise reality, which is to be found in the inner workings of the mind or in some spiritual realm. At others, it has been maintained that truth can be discovered only by objective study of those things that can be felt, tasted, seen, heard, or smelled. To advocates of the latter view, observable details hold the key to truth, while to the former the same details only hide the more significant aspects of truth. Although all writers attempt to depict the truth as they see it, the individual playwright's conception of truth is determined in large part by his basic temperament and talents, and by the religious, philosophical, social, and psychological influences which have shaped them. But, because in each period and movement there are many shared beliefs, we may generalize about the conceptions of truth that provide the raw material of drama and influence the style of that period or movement.

Second, style results from the manner in which the playwright manipulates his means of expression. All dramatists have at their disposal the same basic means—sound and spectacle, or the aural and visual—out of which to create plot, character, and thought. Nevertheless, the work of each playwright is distinctive, for each perceives the human condition from a somewhat different point of view and each must find methods adequate to communicate his vision to others. His perceptions are reflected in the situations, characters, and ideas he invents, in his manipulation of language, and in his suggestions for the use of spectacle. Thus, the playwright who believes that truth is embodied in the details of daily existence will probably invent incidents and characters modeled closely upon contemporary life, and his dialogue, settings, and costumes will mirror faithfully the speech, places, clothing, and behavior of daily existence. On the other hand, the playwright who believes that truth must be sought in some psychological or spiritual realm may depart from the standards of observable reality and may deliberately distort or eliminate details in order to force the audience to look behind surface appearances.

In the theatre, style results from the manner in which the play is presented. The directing, acting, scenery, costumes, lighting, music and dance used to translate the play from the written script to the stage may each be manipulated to affect stylistic qualities. (Each of these elements is treated at length in Part 3 of this book.) Because so many persons are involved in producing a play, it is not unusual to find conflicting or inconsistent stylistic elements in a single production. Normally, however, unity of style is a primary artistic goal. Each theatre artist, working with his own means, seeks to create qualities analogous to those found in the written text, and the director then coordinates all of the parts into a unified whole. On the other hand, plays are sometimes presented in a manner at variance with the script. Such departures, however, are usually made deliberately and for the sake of some effect considered more significant than that which could be achieved by faithfulness to the original text. The Russian director Vsevelod Meyerhold, for example, converted *The Dawns*, a poetic symbolist play of the late nineteenth century, into a piece that reflected the Russian Revolution and even had the latest news dispatches from the battle front inserted into the performance each evening. In such cases, the director becomes the primary creator, and his work is affected by the same determinants that influence the style of a writer.

Ultimately, then, style in drama and theatre results from the way in which means are adapted to ends. It contributes significantly to that sense of unity and wholeness which is the mark of effective drama.

In many contemporary discussions of the theatre, the term *stylization* is used to indicate any deviation from realism. This terminology is sometimes helpful but it is imprecise, since realism is itself a style and since departures from realism may be in any number of directions. Every play has a style, although, as with form, the specific label to be attached to it may be difficult to determine.

Since dramatic structure, form, and style may be combined in infinite variations, discussions of them remain abstract until applied to specific examples. The chapters that follow show how these principles have been put into practice. Each chapter in Part 2 summarizes briefly the development of theatre and drama in a particular era, and outlines the background needed for understanding the plays and theatrical conventions of that period. In addition, in each chapter, one or more representative plays are analyzed and treated both as products of a specific time and place and as art works that transcend their age. Pertinent points about dramatic structure, form, and style are considered when relevant. A chronological order is used because each period is in part an outgrowth of what has gone before. Thus, the historical survey provides a perspective from which to view our present situation.

3

The Performance and the Critic

Watching a live performance of a drama differs radically from reading a script of the same drama. In reading, only two elements are involved: the written word and the readers' capacity to understand and envision what is conveyed through the written word. But a live performance translates the written word into speech and gives concreteness to movement, setting, costume, atmosphere, and all else that must be imagined in a reading. The reader himself is translated into a spectator–auditor, and his solitariness is replaced by a group experience. In fact, a live performance may be thought of as an act of cooperative imagination which extends from the playwright's script through the director's conception of the script (and the interpretations of that conception by actors, designers, musicians, dancers, and technicians) to the audience's perception of the results—the finished production. Because a performance is so much more complex than a script, it is, when all goes well, far more rewarding than a reading and, when things go wrong, far more disappointing. Thus, each production carries with it the potential both of great success and the danger of abysmal failure. Nevertheless, until the transition from script to performance is made, we have not arrived at that collective act we label theatre.

The Production

Like a reading, a production usually has its origins in a script. In fact, in the early stages of his work, a director is merely another reader, and like any reader he seeks to understand and envision the action. If he is to stage the script, he usually must read the play many times, and through some method (perhaps, though not necessarily, the one outlined in the preceding chapter), he analyzes it carefully. Eventually, he arrives at that view (or concept) of the play which he considers most appropriate to the script or to the uses he intends to make of the script. (A director may, if he chooses, depart markedly from the playwright's original conception.) Then, with the aid of actors, designers, and other theatrical personnel, he sets out to embody this concept through a production which can be performed for an audience. What results might be described as one reading (among all those possible) of a script, although one which has been translated into concrete form.

A performance differs from a reading in part, then, in being interpreted from a particular point of view. If the spectator is familiar with the script already, he may recognize that one view has been chosen and others rejected, but often he knows the play only through the performance that is unfolding as he watches. Thus, he may have no fixed point of reference against which to judge how well the performance embodies the script. For this reason, it is often difficult to judge which strengths and weaknesses of a production stem from the script and which from the performance.

Most directors attempt to give a faithful interpretation of the playwright's intentions, but some merely use the script as a point of departure for their own creation. For example, one of Jerzy Grotowski's most famous productions was based on Stanislaw Wyspiański's *Akropolis* (1904), a play set in Cracow, the ancient capital of Poland (and thus the Polish equivalent of the Greek Acropolis). During the action, biblical, classical, and historical figures from the castle's tapestried walls come to life and enact scenes relevant to modern times; eventually all the characters are led by Christ into a future filled with promise and hope. Grotowski transposed the action to the Nazi extermination camp at Auschwitz, where inmates played out grotesque versions of the play's scenes before being led by a lifeless mop-and-rag Christ figure into the ovens. Obviously, Grotowski drastically altered the original work and in doing so created his own commentary on Western culture, values, and future

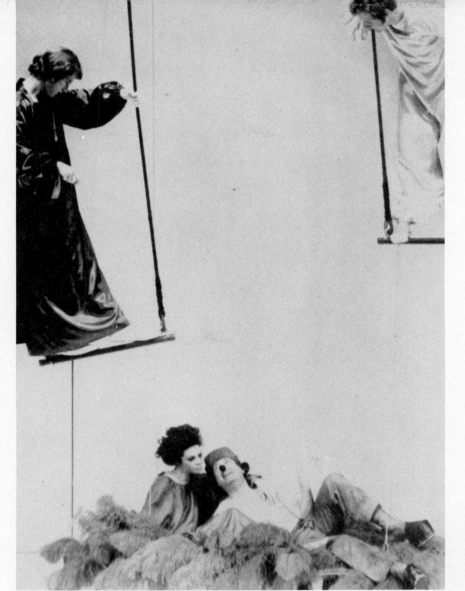

Peter Brook's production of A
Midsummer Night's Dream
*at the Shakespeare Memorial
Theatre, Stratford-on-Avon, in
1970. (Courtesy Royal Shakespeare Company.)*

prospects. While Grotowski's production was powerful, those spectators
without any knowledge of Wyspiański's play were in no position to judge
the changes. In addition, they missed one dimension of the production—
the implied commentary on a Polish classic and Western values.

The relationship of the director's conception to the original script has
been a subject of much debate. Should a director always seek to give a
faithful interpretation of the playwright's script? Or, is a production an
autonomous artistic event that should be viewed independently of the
author's inventions? Critics have argued articulately and persuasively both
negative and positive answers to these questions.

Of course, not all departures from the author's text are so radical as those made in Grotowski's production of *Akropolis*. Sometimes directors believe they must avoid a literal approach to a script in order to focus attention on its essential meanings. This intention seems to have been Peter Brook's motivation in his staging of Shakespeare's *A Midsummer Night's Dream* in 1970. Brook thought Shakespeare's play had not been adequately understood, owing to the traditional emphasis on fantastic and farcical aspects of the story, especially those of the fairy-sprite world. Brook wished instead to make the audience see the play as an exploration of love and the way it can go awry. He used no scenery in the traditional sense, and sought to suggest the magical and fantastic element through devices borrowed from the circus (such as swinging on trapezes and juggling). Shakespeare's text was left intact, and, despite its novelty, Brook's approach managed to focus attention on the script rather than its spectacular trappings.

Many directors argue that to render a text too literally (that is, to adhere too closely to the author's script) may in fact obscure rather than illuminate it, especially if the play is from another time or culture. They believe that the primary challenge is to find a way of bridging the gap between today's audience and the play, whose relevance may not be apparent if it is presented straightforwardly. Thus, in staging Shakespeare's plays it has become common to change the period of the action to one more familiar to the audience or to make other changes designed to create meaningful associations between the sensibilities and values of the present and those depicted in the world of the play. In the hands of sensitive and skilled directors, such transpositions are often extremely effective, but with the less skilled they frequently seem merely eccentric and distracting.

Regardless of what choices have been made, when a play is performed on the stage, the production becomes the concretization of a specific vision of the script. Every aspect of the drama has been envisioned and put in its place, from which it cannot be moved—at least, from the audience's point of view. If this visualization has been done effectively, it frees the spectator from the necessity of imagining everything for himself, for the implications and demands of the script have been given material form. This is not to say that all details have been rendered realistically, but rather that they have been given the form considered appropriate by the director. The concretization of the details (the actions of the characters, how they are dressed, the appearance of the setting, the stage business, the lighting, the tones of voice, and so on) leaves the spectator free to concentrate on the developing action and the relationship among the characters, on the rhythms and the overall meaning of the drama. The spectator is allowed to absorb the play as he would a scene from life, through watching and listening, rather than, as in reading, seeking inwardly both to see and hear everything.

Nevertheless, for an audience performance has its drawbacks. The spectator must allow himself to be carried along at whatever pace the performers set, and if he misses a line or piece of business, he cannot go back and recover it. In the theatre there can be no instant replays. In reading a script, one may encounter a passage that makes one wish to reconsider an earlier scene which has foreshadowed this one and in which the lines must be studied carefully in terms of their precise wording. Or, the reader may find his attitude about a character changing, and he may wish to go back to the beginning of the play to see whether he has missed or misunderstood something there. In other words, a reader may proceed at his own pace, stop and start, turn back or look ahead. Additionally, the reader may decide that there are a number of valid (or possible) alternative interpretations of a line or scene, whereas a director, even if he agrees, must choose one and ignore the others. Play reading, then, is a more flexible activity than play watching, although usually not so satisfying as a truly outstanding performance.

Not all productions, of course, embody adequately their directors' concepts. A director may have had to cast actors not wholly suited to their roles; his designers may not have been able to capture the qualities that he had in mind; and performance conditions may have worked against him. On the other hand, there is no guarantee that a director has understood the text adequately, or if he has, that he is sufficiently skilled to realize his conceptions. In such instances, an imaginative reading of the script may well give more pleasure than a live performance.

What a spectator sees and hears is also affected by the space in which he experiences a performance. Does the theatre have a proscenium-arch stage, a thrust stage, an arena stage? Are the acoustics such that the actors can easily be heard? Are the sight lines such that all the action can easily be seen? Is the seating sufficiently comfortable that one does not become weary? Are the temperature and ventilation adequately controlled? Unless the spectator can hear and see what he should and unless he is freed from distractions, he may be unable to concentrate on the developing action and thus he may miss important moments. Ultimately, it is not enough that a production be thought through and executed carefully; it must also be projected to an audience, without whose comprehension the effort of production has been wasted.

But because theatre is a cooperative art, no member of the team can be compelled to conform to prescribed behavior. Thus, despite the care of director, actors, designers, and technicians, a spectator still may choose to watch characters who are peripheral to a particular moment in the action, or to study the arrangement of the scenery rather than watch the performers, or to survey the audience rather than look at what the director has so carefully planned for him to see. It is the challenge of trying to control the artistic medium and audience response in juxtaposition with the unpredictability of audiences, performers, and equipment (both from moment to moment and from performance to performance) that gives the theatre its special qualities.

Watching a Performance

Just as there are no rules about how to read a play, so too there are none about how to watch a performance. Watching intelligently is primarily a matter of being willing to give one's full attention to what is happening on the stage and of noting meaningful patterns as they emerge. Almost anyone can do it, although clearly some persons derive more from a performance than others. It is assumed that readers of this book will attend the theatre regularly and that as they become more knowledgeable they will find playgoing increasingly rewarding.

Attending a play differs in several ways from going to a film, even though both may take place in a building we call a theatre. Going to a live performance usually has much more of the sense of a special occasion. Except in large cities, live performances are not always available, and one must await the opportunity to attend. One must usually buy tickets in advance and go to the theatre at a specified time since performances are not continuous. The sense of occasion is also evident in the dress of spectators (although less so now than formerly). Since tickets for a live performance usually prescribe the seat in which one must sit, much more

*The audience was elegantly
dressed for this presentation of*
La Princesse de Navarre
*at the Court of Versailles,
in the eighteenth century.
(Culver Pictures)*

attention is paid than at movies to such matters as ushering spectators to their seats. For live performances, spectators are usually provided with programs which give information about the cast, the production staff, and the play.

Since nowadays the stage is seldom hidden by a curtain, the spectator can usually examine the stage and scenery and gain some idea of the production style before the performance begins. Frequently, music is used to help put the audience in the appropriate mood. Most live performances have one or more intermissions, which permit the audience to leave their seats, mingle with each other, and discuss what they have seen or what is to come.

Most of all, however, the live performance differs from film because a play is enacted by live performers in the audience's presence. Therefore, the play unfolds for the spectator at the same time it does for the characters. Members of the audience become participants in an event rather than mere watchers of pictures.

The moment a performance begins, many of the questions a reader must seek to answer are automatically provided. In the preceding chapter, while discussing the problems of reading a play, the opening scene of *Oedipus the King* was cited as an example, and a number of questions about the scene were raised: What does the palace look like? Where are the altars placed? How are the characters dressed? How are they positioned? Do they move? If so, when and in what manner? At what tempo does the scene proceed? What is the tone of the scene? In a performance, these and many other questions are almost instantaneously answered as soon as the play begins, and still others are raised and answered throughout the performance.

The spectator, then, is primarily the receiver of images and sounds created for him by others. Therefore, less imagination is required to see and hear than to read a play. It would be a mistake, however, to think that at a performance no imagination is required. The spectator still must assess what he sees and hears, try to understand the relationship of the characters, and interpret ambiguous speeches or actions.

Unlike a film, in which the setting is usually realistic (often photographed actual places), a live performance may use little scenery. Therefore, the spectator may need to imagine much that is merely suggested by a few set-pieces, projections, lighting effects, or dialogue: the same basic setting may be used to represent a variety of different locales. Costumes also are at times fragmentary; or the performers may appear in ordinary street dress or rehearsal clothing, while the audience is expected to imagine them to be biblical or historical personages. The spectator may be asked to imagine that a character has traveled a great distance even though he has not left the stage, or that considerable time has passed even though no device such as the film's fadeout or rapid cut is used. Often the audience is asked to project itself (or to adapt its mode of seeing) to visual styles or schemes of probability at considerable variance from ordinary experience. These and other conventions may make enormous demands on the spectator's imagination.

In addition to using his imagination, the spectator must be able to concentrate. Unless he watches intently, letting his eye and ear be carried along by whatever devices have been used by the director to achieve emphasis and subordination, he may fail to comprehend what is significant in the complex stage picture, all of which remains visible since the director cannot use closeups, directional shots, or other filmic devices to force the audience to see what he wishes to do.

If we are attentive, the chances are that we will comprehend and enjoy what we see and hear. But that is not necessarily so, for what we are shown may be so strange or so ineptly performed that we fail to take it in. (The functions, goals, working methods, and materials of each of the theatre arts involved in live performance are discussed at length in Part 3 of this book.) If we are to distinguish between when inadequacies lie within us and when they are owing to the performance or the script, we must strive to develop our knowledge and sensibilities.

Every time we read a play or witness a performance we pass some kind of judgment on it, however subjective or fleeting. But, if this judgment is to be more than superficial, we need to develop an informed approach to scripts and performance which will help us to understand them and arrive at judgments about their relative merits by applying appropriate criteria to them. In other words, we must seek to become critics of the theatre.

The Critic

The title of critic is usually reserved for those persons who formulate their judgments for publication. (Sometimes a distinction is drawn between the "reviewer" and the "critic" on the assumption that the former merely reports his impressions of a production immediately after seeing it whereas the latter takes the time to write thoughtful analyses, but in actuality the line between the two is so blurred that the difference is often indistinguishable.) Ideally, the critic should be an experienced and trained audience member who understands plays and theatrical practice well enough to assess effectiveness and who understands his audience well enough to express evaluations in terms comprehensible to it.

Criticism should be illuminating to both the creators and the consumers of a theatre piece. In making explanations or in passing judgments, most critics refer to specific passages in a play, to characterization, structure, acting, or aspects of staging. In this way, they should be of service to the theatre workers as well as to the public by pointing out reasons for success or failure.

But a single piece of criticism will not serve the needs of all persons, for, just as a playwright selects an audience for his work, so too the critic has an audience or type of reader in mind. The reviews of plays published in the New York daily newspapers are addressed to a general public, and almost no background or knowledge is taken for granted. On the other hand, the criticism written for literary quarterlies is addressed to a more sophisticated and selected audience. Therefore, not all criticism can be read in the same way.

Even when the critic's assumptions are clear, however, there is often a wide range of response to his work. One reader will find a piece of criticism illuminating, while another will find nothing of value in it, for just as one is drawn to certain kinds of plays, one is also drawn to particular types of criticism. As with plays, some of which continue to be acted for generations, criticism may also remain illuminating to readers in widely separated times. Most criticism, like most drama, however, speaks for the moment and is then forgotten.

Not everyone need aspire to be a practicing critic (in the sense of writing and publishing his judgments), but everyone interested in the theatre can become a better judge by acquiring the background necessary for an adequate understanding of plays and theatrical performances.

The Meaning and Purposes of Criticism

To many, criticism always implies adverse comments, but its true meaning is "the act of making judgments." Therefore, every evaluation should consider both excellence and failure—the effect and the ineffective—in a play and its production. Criticism has been used for three main purposes: exposition, appreciation or denunciation, and evaluation. A piece of criticism is seldom restricted to one of these purposes; usually all are found in conjunction.

The purpose of expository criticism is to explain a play, circumstances affecting it, or aspects of its production. The critic may write about the author, the period in which he lived, the source of his ideas, and similar factors. Using this approach a critic need make no judgment of worth. For example, he might explain how Shakespeare's *Richard III* is constructed or how the actual events differed from Shakespeare's version, and, although his examination should lead to better understanding of the play, he need not judge its overall effectiveness. Similarly, the reviewer may provide information about certain aspects of a production (the visual appearance of scenery and costumes, how this production differs from previous ones of the same play, and so on) without passing judgment on them. Eventually, he usually feels obliged to state his opinion of the production as a whole, but a large portion of his review may be purely expository.

Appreciative or denunciatory criticism is usually written by the critic who has already decided that a play or production is good or bad. His principal motive then is to make others feel the power or lack of power in

The battle at the Comédie Française between Classicists and Romanticists on the opening night of Victor Hugo's Hernani *(1830). The play's triumph signaled French acceptance of romanticism. (From Frederic Loliée's* La Comédie Française. *Paris, 1907.)*

the play or production. He may proceed by describing his own responses and then attempt to evoke similar feelings in his readers. He may also analyze the play or production to show how its structure, acting, mood, or other elements bear out his judgment.

The evaluative critic may employ exposition, appreciation, or denunciation, but his principal aim is to judge effectiveness. He may begin by analyzing structure, characterization, ideas, language, and visual elements; or he may investigate the author's life or the historical context. Upon this and other evidence, the critic builds his evaluation of the effectiveness of the script. If he is writing about a production, he may explain his understanding of the playwright's intentions and then go on to assess how effectively they have been realized on the stage; or he may concentrate on the acting and evaluate each performer's characterization. However he proceeds, his concern is to provide an evaluation of what he has seen and heard in the theatre.

The Basic Problems in Criticism

In pursuing his work, the serious critic is concerned with three basic problems: understanding, assessing effectiveness, and judging ultimate worth.

In attempting to understand a play, the critic must make sure that all of the important keys to its meaning have been explored. First, he should analyze the play, preferably through a study of the script. But before he can fully understand the script, the critic may need to undertake other explorations. Sometimes a study of the author and his background is essential. If the play is a work from the past, it may be necessary to examine the dominant religious or psychological beliefs of that period, or the staging conventions in vogue when the play was written.

While these are methods used by the literary critic, they are also employed by theatre workers in their study of a script prior to its production. Unless the director, the actors, and the scenic artists understand a drama, it will be difficult for them to produce it satisfactorily. Although the literary critic and the theatre worker may arrive at the same conclusions in their studies, the theatre worker usually finds that his understanding of the play is modified during the rehearsal period. As the play takes shape on stage, he discovers qualities of which he was previously unaware, for plays do not reveal all of their potentialities on the printed page. Conversely, not all of the implications found in a script can be projected to an audience in a single production. Whenever possible a play should be studied both on the printed page and in performance.

Many reviewers write about plays which they have not read and which they know only from a single viewing. Since understanding may be severely limited under such circumstances, most reviewers restrict themselves to reporting impressions without pretending to provide an extensive analysis of the play. Nevertheless, reviewers are sometimes guilty of damning a play rather than its inadequate production or a performance rather than its inadequate script, for it is difficult to sort out the sources of weaknesses or strenghts on the basis of a single viewing.

After a play is understood, it may be judged in terms of how well it fulfills its intentions. Rarely, however, does a playwright state his intentions either within a play or elsewhere. Rather, intention must be determined through probing analysis. It is indicated by such elements as tone (a play may be humorous, satirical, serious, whimsical, and so on), ideas and their treatment, dialogue, characterization, and conflicts. The critic comes to recognize whether the author is attempting to arouse indignation at some social injustice, deriding a political position, merely trying to offer an evening of entertainment, or seeking to accomplish some other purpose. Having decided upon the basic purpose of the play, he can then assess how effectively this purpose has been realized.

Assessment of effectiveness can be based entirely upon a study of the script, but it is helpful and always wise to note the response of audiences to productions of the script. It should be kept in mind, however, that while the response may be an accurate measure of the audience's enjoyment, it will not always give a true indication of the play's potential power. For example, the play may not have been well performed. Or other factors—such as unfamiliar dramatic techniques or complex ideas —may be responsible for an audience's failure to appreciate a play's power. In such cases, the fault does not necessarily lie with the play, but may indicate shortcomings in the audience. But, if the play has been adequately performed and understood, then audience response is helpful in determining whether the intention of the playwright has been achieved. In making his judgment, the wise critic draws on all the resources available to him.

In seeking to assess the effectiveness of a production, the problems are much the same as in judging a script; however, rather than being concerned with the playwright's intention, the critic needs to focus on the director's concept, which may differ radically from what the script seems to demand. Of course, the critic may choose to assess how the director's conception is related to or differs from the playwright's script, but if he is concerned with production as such (rather than as an attempt to embody a script faithfully), he must seek to assess how well the director has achieved what he set out to do. Although he may believe the director to be misguided in his conception, that belief is irrelevant in an assessment of whether or not the concept has been realized. Usually evidence as to the director's intention comes entirely from what the critic sees and hears during the performance, but often the director indicates what his intentions have been through notes in the printed program, interviews given prior to the opening, or publicity releases.

Even though a play or production is understood and judged successful in carrying out its intention, it may still be found unsatisfactory in relation to some larger system of value. Consequently, before passing final judgment, the critic may wish to ask whether the accomplishments are sufficiently significant to merit the highest commendation. It is in making this final judgment that he faces his greatest problem, for there are no universally accepted standards of worth.

To judge a play, it must be surrounded by some larger context which places it in perspective. Disagreements about a play's worth often stem from differences of opinion about the appropriate context. Some critics, for example, argue that the only meaningful context is other plays of the same type; other critics pay little attention to a play's dramatic form but view it within a context of philosophical concepts or of political, social, historical, or economic forces; still others are concerned with psychological forces, ritual elements, or communicative processes. A production may be valued for its novelty, its emotional power, its provocativeness, its relevance, its faithfulness to the script, or its entertainment. The contexts used by modern critics are numerous and varied.

Even though it is impossible to agree upon the single most appropriate context, judgments must be made. Therefore, since a critic cannot force anyone to accept his evaluation, he must rely upon persuasion. Perhaps his first problem is to recognize that his own ingrained convictions and prejudices play an important role in his critical judgments; consequently he should seek to clarify his standards both for himself and for his readers. If he first establishes the criteria by which he is judging a play or production and then states the evidence upon which he bases his judgment, he may persuade others that his is a dependable evaluation.

Because the theatre itself is a composite art and because each of us is subject to many influences, it is difficult to become a good theatre critic. The qualities for which the would-be critic must strive, however, are these: He must be sensitive to feelings, images and ideas; he must become as well acquainted as possible with the theatre of all periods and of all types; he must be willing to explore plays until he understands them thoroughly; he must be tolerant of innovation; he must be aware of his own prejudices and values; he must be articulate and clear in expressing his judgments and their bases. Perhaps most important of all, he must be willing to alter his opinion when new experiences and evidence reveal inadequacies in his earlier judgment, for criticism should be a continuing search rather than the dogmatic defense of a position. Ultimately, it is the purpose of this book to help those who read it to become informed and sensitive critics of plays both as scripts and as performances.

PART 2

THE DEVELOPMENT OF THEATRE AND DRAMA FROM THE BEGINNING UNTIL THE PRESENT

4

Theatre and Drama in Ancient Greece

The Origins of Theatre and Drama

No one really knows how the theatre began, but there are many theories about it. The one most widely accepted today is based upon the assumption that theatre evolved from ritual. The argument for this view goes as follows. In the beginning, human beings viewed the natural forces of the world, even the seasonal changes, as unpredictable, and they sought, through various means, to control these unknown and feared powers. Those measures which appeared to bring the desired results were then retained and repeated until they hardened into fixed rituals. Eventually stories arose which explained or veiled the mysteries of the rites. As humans progressed in knowledge, some rituals, such as those involving human sacrifice, were abandoned, but the stories, later called myths, persisted and provided material for art and drama.

Those who believe that drama evolved out of ritual also argue that primitive rites contained the seeds of theatre because music, dance, masks, and costumes were almost always used. Furthermore, a suitable site had to

be provided for performances, and when the entire tribe did not participate, a clear division was usually made between the "acting area" and the
"auditorium." In addition, there were performers, for, since considerable
importance was attached to avoiding mistakes in the enactment of rites,
priests usually assumed the task for the tribe. Wearing masks and costumes, they often impersonated men, animals, or supernatural beings, and
mimed the desired effect—success in hunt or battle, the coming of rain,
the revival of the sun—as an actor might. From such dramatic rituals,
theatre is said to have emerged as man became sufficiently sophisticated to
separate dramatic from religious activities.

The theory that drama and theatre originated in ritual has much to
recommend it, since it is probably true that unsophisticated peoples do
not distinguish among the various aspects of their lives (work, religion,
play) as clearly as more advanced societies do. The weakness of the
theory lies in the fact that all of man's attempts to deal with his
world (science, philosophy, art) were in the beginning just as much a part
of ritual as theatre was. In seeking to ensure a bountiful harvest, primitive peoples performed rituals (rather than, for example, spreading fer-
tilizer); in these rites they summed up their conception of themselves and
their universe. In most ceremonies, theatrical and dramatic elements were
present. But the theory of ritual origin does not explain why theatre and
drama continued to be valued and to grow in importance after they were
divorced from religious rite and thus lost their former status as effective
means of influencing man's welfare.

Another theory traces the theatre's origin from the human interest in
storytelling. According to this view, tales (about the hunt, war, or other
feats) are gradually elaborated, at first through the use of impersonation,
action, and dialogue by a narrator and then through the assumption of
each of the roles by a different person. A closely related theory traces theatre to those dances that are primarily rhythmical and gymnastic or from
imitations of animal movements and sounds.

Still another theory relates drama and theatre to the human "play" instinct, both in the sense of recreational activity and of playing at being
someone else in a particular activity or situation. This instinct may be
what Aristotle had in mind when he wrote in the *Poetics* that human
beings are instinctively imitative—that they both enjoy imitating others
and seeing imitations, for they desire to know how it would feel to be
another person or why others act as they do. Furthermore, he adds, imitation is one of their chief methods of learning about their world, as when
children learn speech and behavior by imitating adults.

In the twentieth century, a number of psychologists have suggested that
human beings have a gift for fantasy through which they seek to reshape
reality into more satisfying forms than those of daily life. Thus, through
fiction (of which drama is one form) they objectify their anxieties and
fears so that they may confront them or so that they may imaginatively
fulfill their hopes and dreams. Consequently, theatre is one tool whereby

Shrine priest dancing at Bonkwae Brong festival (a traditional religious festival of Ghana). (Photo made in 1970; courtesy Michael Warren.)

humans define and understand their world or one whereby they escape from unpleasant realities.

But while most groups have produced rituals and tales and while man may be an imitator and maker of fantasies, not all societies have produced theatre and drama divorced from ritual. At least two other conditions also seem to be required: a society that can recognize the artistic value of theatre and drama, and individuals capable of organizing theatrical elements into an experience of a high order. For these reasons, the Greeks are usually considered to be the primary originators of drama, for it was they who first developed the form as it was to be known in the Western world.

Egypt and the Near East

Nevertheless, some prior activities deserve brief notice. Ritual probably dates back to the dawn of human history, but our knowledge of it first begins to take definite shape about 4000 B.C., when the civilizations of Egypt and the Near East entered an advanced stage.

Much of our information about the Egyptians is derived from hieroglyphics and artifacts preserved in the pyramids built as tombs for the pharaohs and in the temples of the numerous Egyptian gods. Many of these remains relate to Egyptian myths concerning the recurrent cycle of life and the seasons. In turn, these myths seem to have been utilized in various rituals, about which there has been much controversy concerning the extent to which they were dramatic. Some scholars argue, for example, that the more than fifty surviving "Pyramid Texts" (composed of hieroglyphics and scenes depicting the trials through which the spirit must pass before achieving an honorable place in afterlife) are dramas that were enacted by priests. But, since there is no definitive evidence to support this view, other scholars have denied that the texts are dramatic or that they were ever acted. Other contested rituals relate to the coronation of pharaohs and to the return of spring.

But, in terms of the theatre, the most important of the Egyptian rituals is the so-called Abydos Passion Play, which is concerned with the death and resurrection of the god Osiris. Although it was performed annually from about 2500 to about 550 B.C., no part of the ritual's text remains; all we know of it is deduced from an account left by Ikhernofret, a participant in the ritual some time between 1887 and 1849 B.C. Again, however, scholars differ markedly in their interpretations of Ikhernofret's account. According to some, the ritual was one of the most elaborate spectacles ever staged, including, among other things, battles, processions, and burial ceremonies. Others deny that the life and death of Osiris were reenacted and describe the ritual as a commemoration of all the dead pharaohs and as based on the form of a royal funeral. Considering these opposing views, it is difficult to decide how dramatic or theatrical Egyptian rituals actually were.

In addition to Egyptian rituals, records of others (dating from c. 2500 B.C. onward) in the Near East have been discovered. For the most part, they are concerned with the seasonal pattern of birth, growth, maturity, death, and rebirth. Although some historians have suggested that the rituals of Egypt and the Near East influenced the development of drama in Greece, no direct connection has yet been found. Even if direct influence could be verified, an important difference would still set Greece off from its neighbors. The Egyptians maintained an advanced civilization for about three thousand years (a period longer than that which separates us from the beginnings of Greek drama) and never progressed dramatically beyond ritual. The Greeks, on the other hand, took the steps that established theatre as an autonomous activity. Therefore, it is to Greece that one must look to find the beginnings of the Western tradition in theatre and drama.

The Beginnings of Drama in Greece

For several centuries, Greek drama was presented exclusively at festivals honoring Dionysus, the god of wine and fertility. Supposedly the son of Zeus (the greatest of Greek gods) and Semele (a mortal), Dionysus was killed, dismembered, and then resurrected. Thus, myths about him relate to the life cycle and to seasonal changes: birth, growth, decay, death, and rebirth; spring, summer, fall, and winter. His worship was designed in part to ensure the return of spring and fertility As the god of wine, he also represented many of the world's irrational forces, and his worship was a recognition of man's elemental passions. In the early centuries of Dionysian worship, sexual orgies and drunkenness were accepted parts of the religious impulse, but as time went by these were gradually sublimated, although the basic purpose of Dionysian worship—the inducement of fertility—remained unchanged.

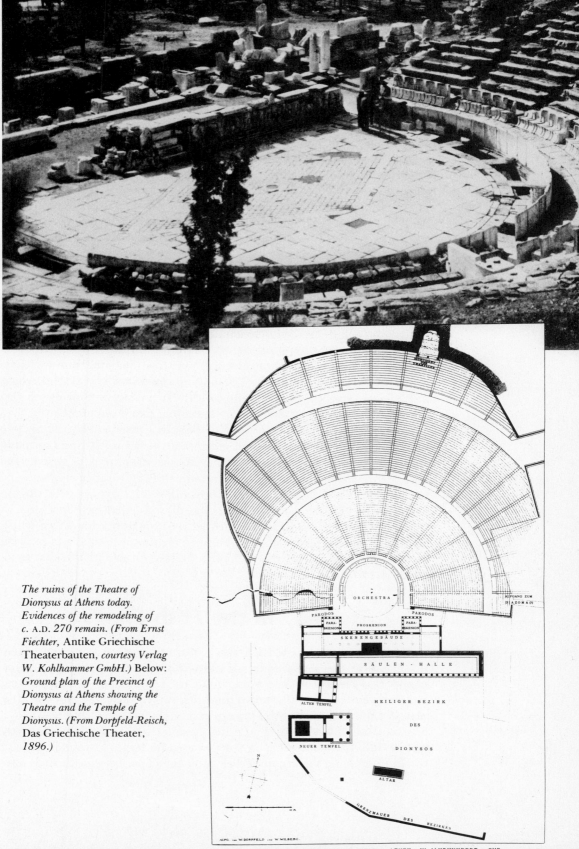

The ruins of the Theatre of
Dionysus at Athens today.
Evidences of the remodeling of
c. A.D. 270 remain. (From Ernst
Fiechter, Antike Griechische
Theaterbauten, courtesy Verlag
W. Kohlhammer GmbH.) Below:
Ground plan of the Precinct of
Dionysus at Athens showing the
Theatre and the Temple of
Dionysus. (From Dorpfeld-Reisch,
Das Griechische Theater,
1896.)

ORCHESTRA

AUFGANG ZUM
(AZOMA (?)

PARODOS   PARODOS
PARA-   PARA-
SKENION   PROSKENION   SKENION
SKENENGEBÄUDE

SÄULEN · HALLE

ALTER TEMPEL

HEILIGER BEZIRK

DES

DIONYSOS

NEUER TEMPEL

ALTAR

N

GRENZMAUER DES BEZIRKES

AUFG. von W.DORPFELD und W.WILBERG.

THEATER UND BEZIRK DES DIONYSOS IN ATHEN. IV. JAHRHUNDERT v. CHR.
ERGÄNZUNG

The inclusion of such irrational forces within the sphere of religion illustrates well the Greek belief that the failure to give due honor to any part of nature can lead to destruction. The Greeks constantly sought to achieve harmony among all conflicting forces, both within and without.

The worship of Dionysus was introduced into Greece from Asia Minor around the thirteenth century B.C., and by the seventh or eighth century B.C., contests of choral dancers were being held at festivals given in his honor. These dances were accompanied by dithyrambs (ecstatic hymns) honoring the god. Aristotle says that it was out of improvisation by the leaders of these hymns and dances that drama developed.

The Greeks did not observe a holy day comparable to our sabbath. Rather, they honored their many gods through religious festivals scattered through the year. By the sixth century B.C., there were four festivals each year in honor of Dionysus alone: the Rural Dionysia (in December); the Lenaia (in January); the Anthesteria (around the end of Feburary); and the City (or Great) Dionysia (around the end of March). Plays were performed at all of these, with the exception of the Anthesteria. Drama was not a part of the festivals held in honor of any other god.

The first definite record of drama in Greece is found in 534 B.C., when the City Dionysia was reorganized and a contest for the best tragedy instituted. Drama probably existed prior to that time, for otherwise a contest would be difficult to explain. The only dramatist of this period whose name has survived is Thespis, who won the first contest. (Since he is also the first known actor, performers are still often called *thespians*.)

The drama of Thespis was relatively simple, since it involved only one actor and a chorus. This does not mean that there was only one speaking character in each play, but rather that all characters were played by the same actor. This single actor used masks in shifting his identity; when he left the stage to change roles, the chorus filled the intervals with singing and dancing. The chorus, therefore, was the principal unifying force in this early drama. Face-to-face conflict between opposing characters, which most later periods have considered a basic feature of drama, was impossible so long as one actor took all roles (unless, of course, the chorus assumed the role of antagonist).

Tragedy in the Fifth Century

Although drama was written and performed in Greece for many centuries, plays by only five writers—Aeschylus, Sophocles, Euripides, Aristophanes, and Menander—now exist. Out of the vast number of plays written, only forty-five survive—thirty-two tragedies, twelve comedies, and one satyr play. All but four of these plays were written during the fifth century.

Aeschylus (525–456) is the earliest dramatist whose plays have survived. He began competing in the contests for tragedy around 499 B.C., but did not win a victory until 484; after that time he won thirteen contests. The titles of seventy-nine of his plays have come down to us but only seven works remain: *The Persians* (472), *Seven against Thebes* (467), the *Oresteia*—a trilogy of plays made up of *Agamemnon, Libation Bearers,* and *Eumenides* (458), *The Suppliants,* and *Prometheus Bound* (exact dates unknown). *The Persians* is unique among surviving Greek dramas in having been based on an historical event (the Persian war) rather than on mythology, although other now-lost plays on historical subjects were written.

Aeschylus' major innovation was the introduction of the second actor, which encouraged face-to-face conflict. The subsequent increase in emphasis on the actor reduced the importance of the chorus, though it remained a dominant force.

The power of Aeschylus' drama can best be appreciated through the only surviving Greek trilogy, the *Oresteia,* one of the great monuments of dramatic literature. As in most of his plays, Aeschylus is concerned here with man's relationship to the gods and the universe and with moral principle. The *Oresteia* dramatizes a development in the concept of justice. In the first two plays the characters conceived of justice as personal revenge, but in the final play, private justice is replaced by the impersonal power of the state. This evolutionary process is demonstrated through a powerful story of murder, reprisal, and remorse, in which the gods participate both directly and indirectly.

Sophocles (496–406) is frequently called the greatest of the Greek dramatists. He is credited with over a hundred plays, of which only seven now exist: *Ajax* (dated variously from 450 to 440), *Antigone* (around 440), *Oedipus the King* (approximately 430 to 425), *Philoctetes* (409), *Electra and Trachiniae* (dates unknown, though considered to be late plays), and *Oedipus at Colonus* (written shortly before Sophocles' death). In addition, a substantial part of *The Trackers,* a satyr play, is extant. He won twenty-four contests, the first in 468 when he defeated Aeschylus. Sophocles introduced a third actor and thus allowed for still greater dramatic complexity than had been possible with two actors. He was much more directly concerned with human relationships than with the religious and philosophical issues which had interested Aeschylus. Furthermore, his dramas place more emphasis upon building skillful climaxes and well-developed episodes than those of Aeschylus, which are sometimes crude in structure. (The qualities of Sophocles' drama will be explored at greater length in the detailed examination of *Oedipus the King*).

Euripides (480–406) was the last of the great Greek tragedians. He is said to have written ninety-two plays, of which seventeen tragedies have survived. Among these the most famous are: *Alcestis* (438), *Medea* (431), *Hippolytus* (428), *Ion,* and *Electra* (dates unknown), *The Trojan Women* (415), and *The Bacchae* (produced after his death). In addition, *The Cyclops* is the only complete satyr play that now exists. Although Euripides achieved great popularity in later times, he was not widely appreciated in his own day, winning only five victories in the tragic contests.

Euripides reduced the role of the chorus in his works until its connection with the rest of the play was often vague. His interests were principally philosophical and psychological. He was a skeptic who questioned many Athenian ideals; even the gods did not escape examination, and in his plays they were frequently made to appear petty and ineffectual; he probed the motives of his characters and found little to admire. He also turned toward melodrama and frequently resorted to contrived endings. Thus he has been admired for his ideas and his psychological realism, but has been criticized for faulty dramatic structure. With his death, the great era of Greek tragedy came to an end.

The Satyr Play

During the fifth century B.C., each writer of tragedy was also required to present a satyr play, along with three tragedies, whenever he competed in the festivals. A satyr play was comic in tone (usually burlesquing a Greek myth) and used a chorus of satyrs. Following the three tragedies, it formed a kind of afterpiece, for it was short and sent the audience home in a happy frame of mind. Since the actors and choruses were the same for both tragedies and satyr play, the conventions of acting, costuming, and scenery were probably similar for both forms, although they were given a marked satirical turn in the satyr plays.

Only one complete satyr play—the *Cyclops* by Euripides—still exists. Like all satyr plays, it is divided into five sections by four choral odes after the manner of tragedy and is a parody of a serious story—in this instance, Odysseus' encounter with the Cyclops. A substantial part of one

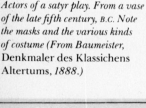

Actors of a satyr play. From a vase of the late fifth century, B.C. Note the masks and the various kinds of costume (From Baumeister, Denkmaler des Klassichens Altertums, *1888.)*

other satyr play—*The Trackers* by Sophocles—is also extant. It deals with Apollo's attempts to recover a herd of cattle stolen from him by Hermes and has the same structural features as the *Cyclops*. Although the satyr play was a regular feature of the Athenian theatre of the fifth century, it has had little subsequent influence and ceased to exist as a form when Greek drama declined.

Play Production

Greek drama can best be appreciated through a detailed examination of a representative play. For this purpose *Oedipus the King* has been chosen. But, since information about the theatrical conventions for which it was written will contribute much to our understanding of the play, it will be helpful first to explore the practices that prevailed around 430 B.C., the approximate time when Sophocles' play was first performed.

It was at the City Dionysia, one of the great religious and civic occasions of the year, that *Oedipus the King* was first presented. If a tragic dramatist wished to enter plays at the City Dionysia, he applied to the principal civic magistrate (the *archon eponymous*) for a chorus. We do not know how this official decided among the applicants, but three tragic writers were granted choruses at each City Dionysia.

The magistrate also appointed the *choregoi,* or wealthy citizens who bore the expense of the choruses. One *choregus* was appointed for each dramatist, and the *choregoi* and playwrights were then matched by lot. *Choregoi* for the next City Dionysia were appointed approximately one month after the conclusion of the preceding City Dionysia. This would have allowed almost a year for planning and rehearsal, although not all of this time may have been used.

The *choregus* paid for the training of the chorus, their costumes, the musicians, the supernumerary actors and their costumes, and perhaps for the scenery. In other words, he was responsible for everything except the theatre and the speaking actors. Since he might be either generous or miserly, the *choregus* could seriously affect the playwright's chances of mounting his play satisfactorily. Usually, however, the *choregus* looked upon the proper outfitting of his plays as a civic duty and as a matter of personal pride.

If a playwright were granted a chorus, he was required to present three tragedies and a satyr play. With rare exceptions, the playwright also directed his own works and was in charge of the production as a whole. Until the time of Sophocles the playwright acted in his own plays as well. For his efforts, the playwright was no doubt given some financial remuneration by the state and there was a prize for the winner of the contest, but the amount of money a playwright might receive for his work is unknown. It is extremely doubtful, however, that any of the Greek dramatists of the fifth century earned a living from work as a writer. (Most were from well-to-do families and most probably did not consider playwriting their primary profession.)

The state paid the actors and supplied their costumes; it also furnished the theatre in which the plays were performed. Dramatic production in the fifth century, thus, was financed either by wealthy citizens or by the state, and was looked upon as a religious and civic function of major importance.

The City Dionysia, at which the plays were produced, was considered so important that during it no legal proceedings were allowed and prisoners were released. It opened with a procession in which the statue of the god Dionysus was taken from his temple at the foot of the Acropolis and carried outside the city. His original entry into Athens was then reenacted in a procession that included much revelry. The ceremony concluded with a sacrifice to the god.

The next principal feature of the festival was the performance of *dithyramb*s (hymns to Dionysus sung and danced by choruses of fifty). There were ten choruses each year, five with men and five with boys. Next came the contest for comedies, five probably given on a single day; this was followed by three days devoted to tragedies. On each of these days, three tragedies and a satyr play were performed. After the festival ended, there was a day devoted to evaluating the festival and receiving complaints about its conduct or the misbehavior of citizens during the festival.

To this civic and religious celebration everyone was welcome. Admission was probably free originally, but was later set at the small sum of two *obols,* and even then a public fund was established to provide tickets for those who could not afford the price of admission. The theatre was considered to be the right of everyone rather than a function for the few. Audiences took a keen interest in the contests. In the fifth century, prizes were awarded at each City Dionysia for the best plays (there was a prize for the best comedy and for the best group of tragedies, the honor being shared by the playwright and the choregus), to the best tragic actor, and to the best dithyrambic choruses. The state supervised the judging, and elaborate precautions were taken to insure the secrecy of voting.

The Theatre of Dionysus

At Athens plays were presented in the Theatre of Dionysus situated on the slope of the Acropolis above the Temple of Dionysus. This theatre underwent many changes. In the sixth century it consisted of the hillside on which the spectators stood or sat, and a flat terrace at the foot of the hill for the performers. In the middle of this terrace or *orchestra* (the "dancing place") was an altar (or *thymele*). There probably was no scenic background. Seats, forming an auditorium or *theatron* (the "seeing place"), were gradually added for spectators.

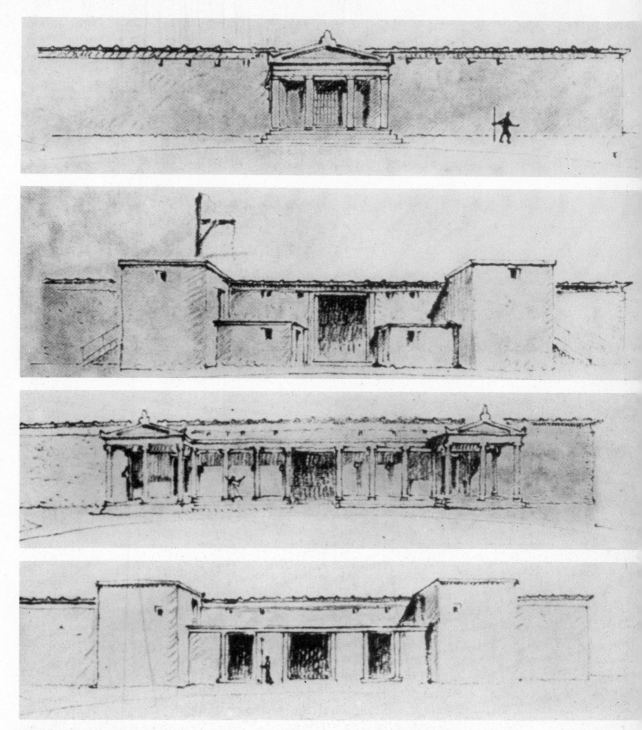

Drawings by Ernst Fiechter of varying conceptions of the stage house for the theatre of Dionysus in the fifth century B.C. (From Fiechter, Antike Griechische Theaterbauten, *courtesy Verlag W. Kohlhammer GmbH, Stuttgart.)*

A conjectural reconstruction of
the stage of the Theatre of
Dionysus remodeled to conform to
the Hellenistic ideal about 150
B.C. (From Fiechter.)

During the fifth and fourth centuries this basic structure was elaborated: a scene house was added and the whole theatre was reconstructed in stone, although this process was not completed until well into the fourth century. The auditorium was the first part of the theatre to assume permanent form when stadiumlike seating was provided by setting stones into the hillside. The semicircular auditorium, which seated about 14,000 persons, curved around the circular orchestra, which measured about sixty-five feet in diameter.

The stage house (or *skene*) was late in developing as a part of the theatre. It was the last part to be constructed in stone, and was remodeled many times after that. For all of these reasons, it is difficult to get a clear impression of the scenic background of plays in the fifth century. The *skene* was originally a place where actors might dress and retire to change roles. Gradually this house came to be used as a background for the action of the play, and its usefulness for scenic purposes was exploited. At the time when *Oedipus the King* was first performed the *skene* was probably a long building which, with its projecting side wings (called *paraskenia*), formed a rectangular background for the orchestra on the side away from the spectators. It was not joined to the auditorium, and the space on each side between the *paraskenia* and the auditorium provided entrances into the orchestra. These entrances were called *parodoi*. (For a plan of the theatre as a whole see the illustration on page 81.)

The appearance of the skene is much debated. Most of the plays are set before temples or palaces, but some take place outside of caves or tents or in wooded landscapes. Consequently, there is much disagreement over the extent to which the background may have been altered to meet these differing demands.

Most scholars believe that the same formalized background was used for all plays. Others, however, argue that, since it was not entirely permanent, the appearance of the skene could have been changed from year to year or from play to play. They point to a series of holes that have been discovered forward of the *skene* foundations and suggest that these could have been used to support upright timbers to which scenery was attached, and that such an arrangement would have facilitated rapid changes in the scenic background. It is impossible to know the truth, but, considering the lack of realistic detail in the plays, it seems unlikely that the Greek ever attempted to create the illusion of a real place in their theatre. Some indication of a play's setting, however, may have been attempted at times through scenic devices.

It is unclear whether there was a raised stage in the theatre of the fifth century, for there is not enough evidence to settle the question definitely. Since the plays seem to require that the actors and the chorus mingle freely, if a platform were used it was probably low enough to allow free access between stage and orchestra. If there were no stage, both the chorus and actors would have used the acting area composed of the orchestra and the rectangular space formed by the scene house. The roof of the stage house also could be used as an acting area.

Since the number of stage entrances varies from play to play, some difference of opinion has arisen about how many doors there were in the stage house. It has become customary to state that there were three in the *skene* and one in each of the *paraskenia,* but in actuality the number is far from certain. Most frequently the actors entered from the stage house, while the chorus used the *parodoi.* There are examples, however, of the chorus entering from the stage house, and of actors using the *parodoi.*

When the available information about the Greek theatre is assembled, a fairly clear picture of its basic structure emerges, but the details of the scenic background remain unclear. (A number of reconstructions of the *skene,* showing variations on many possible features, may be seen on page 00).

While most of the action of Greek plays takes place out of doors, occasionally interiors are indicated. For example, most deaths occur offstage, but the bodies are frequently displayed afterward. For this purpose the large central doorway seems to have been opened and a wheeled platform moved forward. This device is called an *eccyclema* or *exaustra.*

Another effect frequently demanded in Greek plays is the appearance of gods. These characters may descend to the orchestra level or be lifted up from the orchestra to the roof of the stage house. For this purpose, a cranelike device called the *machina* was used. The overuse of gods to resolve difficult dramatic situations led to the expression *deus ex machina* to describe any contrived ending. The eccyclema and the machina are the only two machines that can definitely be ascribed to the fifth century, and these were not used extensively.

It is possible, however, that *periaktoi* were also in use, although these probably belong to a later period. *Periaktoi* are constructed of three flats put together to form a triangle; the triangle is then mounted on a central pivot. Since each surface can be exposed or concealed as desired, it may be used for sudden revelations or for changes in the background.

The Actor

From the time of Sophocles onward, the number of speaking actors in Greek tragedy seems to have been restricted to three, although there might be *extras* who were not considered to be actors. In the second half of the fifth century the state supplied three speaking actors for each tragic playwright competing in the contests. A principal actor was assigned to each playwright by lot. The playwright and his leading actor probably chose the other two actors. All were male and all acted in each of the four plays presented by the same dramatist. Since there were only three actors, each might be asked to play a number of roles.

The style of acting cannot be determined. The plays themselves call for simple realistic actions (such as weeping, running, and falling to the ground). On the other hand, many elements argue against any marked realism. The fact that the same actor played many roles and that men assumed women's parts suggests that realism was not a primary concern. Furthermore, some plays could be performed by three actors only if the same role were played by a different actor in different scenes of the play.

Terracotta figure of an actor found in an Athenian grave; probably fourth century B.C. (Courtesy of the Metropolitan Museum of Art, Rogers Fund, 1913.)

The Greek comic actor and his costume. Terracotta statuette from an Athenian grave c. fourth century B.C. (Courtesy of the Metropolitan Museum of Art, Rogers Fund, 1913.)

The large musical element, the use of dance, and the rather abstract treatment of the story also argue against a realistic style of acting. Nevertheless, the performances should not be thought of as devoid of clearly identifiable human actions. The details of daily life were stripped away but the action did not become so abstract that the audience could not sympathize with the characters. The style suggested by the scripts may be characterized as simple, expressive, and idealized.

Costume

A precautionary note seems necessary at this point. Many theatre historians have failed to distinguish between the practices of the fifth century and those of later Greek times. Nowhere is the failure more misleading than in the treatment of costumes. Frequently the tragic actor is depicted as wearing a high headdress, a mask with distorted features, thick-soled boots, and padded clothing. This costume may have been typical of later periods, but has little to do with the practices of the fifth century, the more typical features of which are outlined below and shown in the accompanying illustrations.

All the actors in Greek tragedy wore masks constructed of lightweight linen, cork, or wood. There were several reasons for this practice: Each actor played a number of roles; all the actors were male though many of the characters were female; the range of age and character types played by a single actor was great. (There is little evidence to support the argument sometimes advanced that the mask acted as a megaphone for the voice.) Although the mouths were open, the features were not exagger-

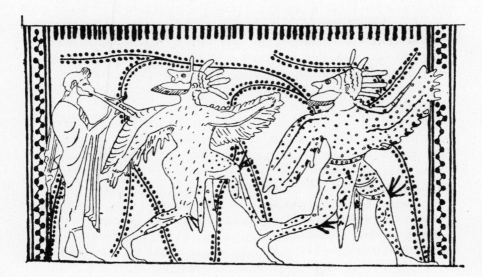

Greek Bird costumes probably similar to those used in Old Comedy. (From Dieterich, Pulcinella, *1897.)*

ated to any marked degree. Headdresses seem to have followed relatively closely those normally worn during the period.

A variety of clothing was used for stage purposes. A long-sleeved, ankle-length, heavily embroidered tunic, or *chiton*, was worn by certain characters, and some historians have argued that it was used for all the principal roles of tragedy. Since some plays contain references to mourning dress, to ragged garments, and to distinctions in clothing between Greeks and foreigners, however, it seems likely that costumes varied considerably. It may be that the sleeved, embroidered tunic (which was not worn in Greek daily life), was reserved for supernatural and non-Greek characters, while native dress was used for others. An ankle-length or knee-length chiton was the usual daily dress in Greece. The selection of the costume was probably determined at least in part by its appropriateness to the role. The tragic actor usually wore a soft, flexible, high-topped boot in common use at that time.

While the actor's appearance was somewhat changed by his costume from what would have been considered normal in that period, he remained relatively undistorted in terms of size and shape. His costume allowed for freedom of movement and speech and facilitated the rapid change of roles.

The Chorus, Music, and Dance Music

Although tradition has it that the tragic chorus originally consisted of fifty members, was later reduced to twelve, and then raised to fifteen, there is little evidence to substantiate any of these figures. Nevertheless, it is generally assumed that during Sophocles' lifetime the chorus was composed of fifteen persons. Usually the chorus performed in unison, but at times it was divided into two semichoruses of seven members; these semichoruses might perform in turn or might exchange or divide speeches. The chorus leader sometimes had solo lines, but the chorus probably spoke and sang as a group (though some modern editions of the plays divide the speeches and assign them to individual chorus members). The chorus usually makes its entrance after the prologue (or opening scene) and except in rare cases remains until the end of the play.

The chorus serves many functions. First, it is an actor in the drama. It expresses opinions, gives advice, and sometimes threatens to interfere in the events of the play. As a rule, it is sympathetically allied with the protagonist. Second, the chorus often establishes the ethical framework of the play. It may express the author's views and set up a standard against which the actions of the characters can be judged. Third, the chorus is frequently the ideal spectator, reacting to the events and characters as the author would like his audience to respond. Fourth, the chorus helps to set the mood of the play and to heighten its dramatic effects. For example, a

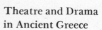

A performance of Oedipus the King *by the Greek National Theatre at Epidaurus. Directed by Alexis Minotis (Photo courtesy of the Greek National Theatre.)*

an interpretation, while it shifts the emphasis somewhat, does not contradict the picture of humans as victims of forces beyond their control, no matter by what name we call those forces.

Another implication, which may not have been a conscious one with Sophocles, is that Oedipus is a scapegoat. The city of Thebes will be saved if the one guilty man can be found and punished. Oedipus, in a sense then, takes the sins of the city upon himself, and in his punishment lies the salvation of others. Thus, Oedipus becomes a sacrificial offering to the gods. There is a parallel here with the crucifixion of Christ, the sacrificial lamb offered up for the sins of all those who believe in Him. This parallel cannot be extended very far, however, since there are more points of difference than of similarity in the two figures.

Another motif—blindness versus sight—is emphasized in poetic images and in various overt comparisons. A contrast is repeatedly drawn between the physical power of sight and the inner sight of understanding. For example, Tiresias, though blind, can see the truth which escapes Oedipus, while Oedipus, who has penetrated the riddle of the Sphinx, cannot solve the puzzle of his own life. When it is revealed to him, he blinds himself in an act of retribution.

These themes indicate that *Oedipus the King* is a comment in part on humankind's relationship to the gods and on humans' attempt to control their own destiny. While the Greek views of these problems may not be ours, the problems and many of the implications are still vital and meaningful.

Plot and Structure. The skill with which *Oedipus the King* is constructed can be appreciated if we compare the complex story (which actually begins with a prophecy prior to the birth of Oedipus) with Sophocles' ordering of the events. In the play there is a simultaneous movement backward and forward in time as the revelation of the past moves Oedipus ever nearer to his doom in the present.

The division of the play into a prologue and five espisodes separated by choral passages is typical of Greek tragedy. The prologue is devoted principally to exposition: a plague is destroying the city of Thebes; Oedipus promises to help and explains the action already taken; Creon returns from Delphi with a command from the Oracle to find and punish the murderer of Laius; Oedipus promises to obey the command. Thus, all of the necessary information is given in a very brief scene, and the first important question (Who is the murderer of Laius?) is raised. The prologue is followed by the *parados*, or entry of the chorus and the first choral slong, in which the plight of Thebes is restated and prayers for deliverance are offered to the gods.

The first episode begins with Oedipus' proclamation and his curse upon the murderer. This proclamation has great dramatic power because Oedipus is unknowingly pronouncing a curse upon himself. Then Tiresias, the seer, enters. It is important to remember that Oedipus has sent for Tiresias on the advice of Creon, since otherwise Oedipus' suspicion of conspiracy between Creon and Tiresias is not understandable. Tiresias' refusal to answer questions provokes Oedipus' anger, the first display of a response which is developed forcefully throughout the first four episodes. It is his quick temper, we later discover, that caused Oedipus to kill Laius. By the time Tiresias has been driven to answer, Oedipus suspects some trickery. This complication is necessary, for had Oedipus summoned Tiresias, heard his story, and believed him, the play would be over. Sophocles has boldly brought out the truth but has cast doubt upon it, for, as Oedipus points out, if Tiresias knew the truth why did he not speak out at the time of Laius' murder? The scene ends in a stalemate of accusations.

It is interesting to note that while all of the first four episodes move forward in the present, they go successively further backward in time. This first episode reveals only that part of the past immediately preceding Oedipus' arrival at Thebes.

The choral passage which follows the first episode reflects upon the previous scene, stating the confusion which Sophocles wishes the audience to feel. The chorus ends by declaring that since Oedipus has saved the city in the past it will continue to have faith in him until he is proven wrong.

The second episode builds logically on the first. Creon comes to defend himself from the accusation that he has conspired with Tiresias. Oedipus, however, is not open to reason. Jocasta is drawn to the scene by the quarrel and she and the chorus persuade Oedipus to abate his anger. This quarrel illustrates Oedipus' complete faith in his own righteousness, since despite Tiresias' accusation, no suspicion of his own guilt has entered his mind. Ironically, it is Jocasta's attempt to placate Oedipus that leads to his first suspicion about himself. She tells him that oracles are not to be believed and as evidence points to Laius' death, which did not come in the manner prophesied. But her description recalls to Oedipus the circumstances under which he has killed a man. He insists that Jocasta send for the one survivor of Laius' party. Thus, a considerable change occurs within this scene—Oedipus' self-righteousness is shaken, and the possibility of his involvement creates additional suspense. The scene also continues the backward exploration of the past, for Oedipus tells of his life in Corinth, his visit to the Oracle of Delphi, and the murder of the man who is later discovered to have been Laius.

The choral song which follows is concerned with the questions Jocasta has raised about oracles. The chorus concludes that if oracles are proven untrue, then the gods themselves are to be doubted. The song, while reflecting upon the scene immediately past, looks forward to a solution of the question.

Oedipus the King directed by Tyrone Guthrie, 1955. Center: Douglas Campbell as Oedipus. Rear: Eleanor Stuart as Jocasta, Robert Goodier as Creon. (Production photo by Donald McKague, courtesy of the Stratford Shakespearean Festival Foundation of Canada.)

Though Jocasta has called oracles into question, she obviously does not disbelieve in the gods themselves, for at the beginning of the third episode she makes offerings to them. She is interrupted, however, by the entrance of the Messenger from Corinth, who brings news of the death of Oedipus' supposed father, Polybus. But this news, rather than arousing grief, as one would expect, is greeted with rejoicing, for it seems to disprove the oracle which had predicted that Oedipus would kill his father. This seeming reversal only serves to heighten the effect of the following events. Oedipus still fears returning to Corinth because the oracle also has prophesied that he will marry his own mother. Thinking that he will set Oedipus' mind at ease, the Messenger reveals that he himself brought Oedipus as an infant to Polybus. The circumstances under which the Messenger acquired the child bring home the truth to Jocasta. This discovery leads to a complete reversal for Jocasta, for the oracles she has cast doubt upon in the preceding scene have suddenly been vindicated. She strives to stop Oedipus from making further inquiries, but he interprets her entreaties as fear that he may be of humble birth. Jocasta goes into the palace; it is the last we see of her, although her actions are later revealed. This scene has not only revealed the truth to Jocasta, it has also diverted attention from the murder of Laius to the birth of Oedipus. It goes backward in time to the infancy of Oedipus. Only one step remains.

The choral song which follows is filled with fanciful hopes, as the chorus speculates on Oedipus' parentage and suggests such possibilities as Apollo and the nymphs. The truth is deliberately kept at a distance here in order to make the following scene more powerful. These speculations, however, do serve to concentrate attention on the question while diverting it from the right solution.

This extremely brief choral song is followed by the entry of the Herdsman (the sole survivor of Laius' party at the time of the murder and the person from whom the Corinthian Messenger had acquired the infant Oedipus). The Herdsman does not wish to speak, but he is tortured by Oedipus' servants into doing so. In this very rapid scene everything that has gone before is brought to a climax. We are taken back to the beginning of the story (Oedipus' birth), we learn the secret of his parentage, we see the truth of the oracle, we find out who murdered Laius, we discover that Oedipus is married to his own mother. The climax is reached in Oedipus' cry of despair and disgust as he rushes into the palace. The brief choral song which follows comments upon the unpredictability of fate and points to Oedipus' life as an example.

The final episode is divided into two parts. A Messenger enters and describes what has happened offstage. The "messenger scene" is a standard part of Greek drama, since Greek sensibilities dictate that scenes of extreme violence take place offstage, although the results of the violence (the bodies of the dead, or in this case Oedipus' blindness) might be shown. It is doubtful, however, that spectators of any age could witness without revulsion the sight of Oedipus jabbing pins into his eyes. Following the messenger scene, Oedipus returns to the stage and seeks to prepare himself for the future.

Oedipus the King is structurally unusual, for the resolution scene is the longest in the play. Obviously, Sophocles was not primarily concerned with discovering the murderer of Laius, for the interest in this lengthy final scene is shifted to the question: What will Oedipus do now that he knows the truth?

Up to this scene the play has concentrated upon Oedipus as the ruler of Thebes, but in the resolution Oedipus as a man and a father becomes the center of interest. By this point he has ceased to be the ruler of Thebes and has become the lowest of its citizens, and much of the intense pathos is due to this change. An audience may feel for Oedipus the outcast as it never could feel for the self-righteous ruler shown in the prologue.

Oedipus' act of blinding himself grows believably out of his character, for it is his very uprightness and deep sense of moral outrage that causes him to punish himself so terribly. Although he is innocent of intentional sin, he considers the deeds themselves (murder of a blood relative and incest) to be so horrible that ignorance cannot wipe away the moral stigma. Part of the play's power resides in the revulsion with which people in all ages have viewed patricide and incest. That they are commited by an essentially good man only make them more terrible.

Oedipus the King maintains completely the unities of action, time, and place. There is nothing in the play that is not immediately relevant to the story being told. There are no subplots, and even the main plot it treated as simply as its events will allow. The time that elapses in the play coincides with the amount of time it would take in performance, and all of the events occur in the same place. The play, thus, has a late point of attack and shows only the final stages of the story. Out of very simple means, the playwright created a drama of concentrated and powerful effect.

Characters and Acting. Sophocles pays little attention to the physiological level of characterization. The principal characters—Oedipus, Creon, and Jocasta—are mature persons, but Sophocles indicates almost nothing about their ages or appearances. One factor which is apt to distract modern readers—the relative ages of Jocasta and Oedipus—is not even mentioned by Sophocles, for it is basically unimportant. According to legend, Jocasta was queen of Thebes when Oedipus answered the riddle of the Sphinx. His reward, being made king, carried with it the stipulation that he marry Jocasta. Sophocles, it should be noted, never questions the suitability of the marriage on the grounds of disparity in age.

Although Sophocles does not dwell on the physical attributes of his major characters, he does give brief indications of age for other roles. The Priest of the Prologue is spoken of as being old; the Chorus is made up of Theban Elders; Tiresias is old and blind; the Herdsman is an old man. In almost every case, age is associated with wisdom and experience. On the other hand, there are a number of young characters, none of whom

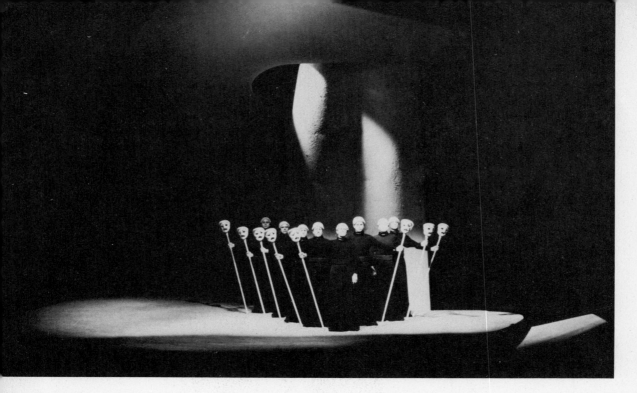

Scene from Oedipus the King *as performed at the Landestheater, Darmstadt, in 1952. Directed by G. R. Sellner, designed by Fritz Mertz. (Photo by Pit Ludwig. Courtesy of the exhibition,* The New Theatre in Germany, *circulated by the Smithsonian Institution.)*

speaks: the band of suppliants in the Prologue includes children, the Antigone and Ismene are very young. Here, the innocence of childhood is used to arouse pity.

On the second level of characterization (social position or class), Sophocles again indicates little. Oedipus, Creon, and Jocasta hold joint authority in Thebes, although the power has been delegated to Oedipus. Vocational designations—a priest, a seer, a herdsman, servants—are used for some of the characters.

Sophocles is principally concerned with psychological and ethical characteristics. For example, we never know how old Oedipus is, but we learn about his moral uprightness, his reputation for wisdom, his quick temper, his insistence on discovering truth, his suspicion, his love for his children, his strength in the face of disaster. It is through these qualities that we come to understand Oedipus. But even here, a very limited number of traits, only those necessary to the story, are shown.

Creon is given even fewer characteristics. He has been Oedipus' trusted friend and brother-in-law, and is one of the rulers of Thebes. Quick to defend his honor, he is a man of common sense and uprightness who acts as honorably and compassionately as he can when the truth is discovered. Jocasta is similarly restricted. She strives to make life run smoothly for Oedipus, she tries to comfort him, to mediate between him and Creon, to stop Oedipus in his quest; she commits suicide when the truth becomes clear. We know nothing of her as a mother, and the very existence of the children is not mentioned until after her death.

This treatment of character—the use of few but essential traits—is another sign of Sophocles' economy in writing. His methods are quite unlike those of modern realistic playwrights who tend to build character out of a large number of small details.

In the first production of *Oedipus the King,* all of the speaking roles would have been taken by three actors. The most likely casting would be as follows: The first actor would play Oedipus throughout, since he is present in every scene; the second actor would play Creon and the Messenger from Corinth; the third actor would play the Priest, Tiresias, Jocasta, the Herdsman, and the second Messenger. The greatest range is required of the third actor, while the greatest individual power is required of the first. The demands made on the third actor raises questions about the degree to which he differentiated between characters and the importance masks and costumes played in keeping characters separated for the audience. One should remember, however, that no two of the roles played by the third actor closely resemble each other and that the separation in terms of type might make his task simpler than it at first appears.

In addition to the three speaking actors, a large number of supernumeraries is required, many of whom no doubt appeared in more than one scene. For example, the band of suppliants in the Prologue includes children, two of whom could later appear as Antigone and Ismene. Some who portrayed suppliants probably also appeared later as servants and attendants. To the actors must be added the chorus of fifteen members. Therefore, the total number in the cast was probably not less than thirty-five.

Just as the details of characterization are few, so too the kinds of actions required of the actors are restricted. The physical movement specifically demanded by the script is slight: entering, exiting, kneeling, pouring of sacrificial offerings, torturing the Herdsman, and displays of anger. The use of masks, the doubling of roles, the fact that Jocasta was played by a man, the relatively small range of action—all these factors suggest that, while the aim was to create moving representations of human actions, the overall effect would be considerably more abstract than the acting normally seen in the modern theatre.

Setting, Spectacle, Music, and Dance. The reader used to all the stage directions given in modern scripts may find a Greek tragedy lacking in spectacle upon first reading. If he tries to envision the action as it unfolds moment by moment, however, quite a different impression results.

First of all, the Greek theatre had no curtain. The play begins, therefore, with the procession of the suppliants through one of the *parodoi.* Oedipus arrives to hear their pleas; then Creon enters. Later the suppliants leave, and immediately the Chorus enters with a song which is accompanied by music and dance. This simple outline of the prologue and *parodos* is indicative of the complexity and variety found throughout the play.

The setting of *Oedipus the King* is simple. The stage house represents a palace; no changes are made and no machinery is needed. Relatively few of the characters enter from the palace: Oedipus, Jocasta, the second Messenger, Antigone, Ismene, and sometimes Creon. Most of the characters, however, enter either through the *parodoi* or from the *paraskenia*. The Chorus and the suppliants would also enter through the *parodoi* and would perform in the orchestra.

There would be an altar in the middle of the orchestra, but there would also be altars near the stage house upon which Jocasta could place her offerings. Since the play was performed out of doors in daylight, no artificial illumination was necessary.

Costumes also would add to both setting and spectacle. Since most of the characters, including the Chorus, are dignified Greek citizens, they probably would wear long *chitons*. But there would also be many distinctions among the characters. Suppliants would carry branches as symbols; the Priest, Tiresias, and the Herdsman would wear garments indicative of their occupations. The rich costumes of Oedipus, Jocasta, and Creon would contrast effectively with the simpler garments of the servants. Each actor would wear a mask indicative of his age and character.

Choral dancing is an important element of the spectacle. Since dance had ethical connotations for the Greeks, that used in *Oedipus the King* would have been in keeping with the moral position represented by the chorus of the play. Since the Chorus is made up of elderly, wise men, whatever dance they performed must have been dignified and stately, and

A nineteenth-century reconstruction of a Greek Comedy. (Culver Pictures.)

probably appealed as much through shifting patterns as through dance steps.

103
Theatre and Drama
in Ancient Greece

The aural appeals were several: instrumental music, singing, and the speech of actors. The Greeks placed great emphasis on effective oral delivery. The actors' voices, therefore, must have been well trained, and no doubt they created considerable aural beauty. Plays were performed with musical accompaniment. Occasionally, music was used during the episodes, but normally it was reserved for choral passages, all of which were sung and danced to flute music. Not only does music offer an appeal in its own right, it is also helpful in staging choral interludes, for it makes singing and dancing in unison much easier. Furthermore, music, through volume and tempo, aids in building choral passages to a climax. Movement, music, and song were combined to make the choral interludes among the most striking and effective features of Greek tragedy.

When the dramatic, visual, and musical appeals of Greek drama are considered, it becomes easier to understand why these plays, even after the passage of 2500 years, are still powerful and meaningful works of art.

Comedy

Greek comedy developed later than tragedy did. It was not officially recognized as a part of the festivals—that is, it was not granted a chorus—until about 487 B.C., when it became a regular feature of the City Dionysia. After 487, one day of each festival was devoted to the presentation of five comedies. At the City Dionysia, however, comedy was always considered inferior to tragedy; it was to find its true home at the Lenaia—the January Dionysian festival—at which it was given official state support beginning around 442 B.C. At the same time, contests for both comic poets and comic actors were inaugurated there. The festival arrangement and the production procedures were similar to those for the City Dionysia, though the Lenaia festival was less elaborate. Five comic poets competed at the Lenaia, as at the City Dionysia. After 432, two tragic dramatists provided two tragedies each year as well. Satyr plays and dithyrambs were never presented at the Lenaia.

Comedy used a chorus of twenty-four members, which like the tragic chorus might be divided into two semichoruses. The chorus also sang and danced and served the same functions as the tragic chorus, but its music and dance were directed, as a rule, toward creating comic effects, although Aristophanes frequently inserted beautiful lyrical choruses into his comedies.

The most typical costumes seems to have been a very tight, too-short *chiton* worn over flesh-colored tights, which created a ludicrous effect of partial nakedness. This effect was further emphasized by the *phallus* (male sexual organ), which was attached to the costumes of most male characters. The phallus was both a source of ribald humor and a constant reminder of the Dionysian purpose of the festival. Masks also were used to emphasize the ridiculous appearance of the characters. (See the illustrations).

Occasionally comic masks were used to depict actual persons. For example, when *The Clouds* was first produced Socrates is said to have stood up in the theatre so the audience might compare the actor's mask with his own facial features. Other masks and costumes created appropriate (though not necessarily realistic) likenesses for the nonhuman choruses —of birds, frogs, clouds, wasps, and so on—that abound in Old Comedy.

Principally, however, comedy differed from tragedy in its subject matter. Most typically it was concerned with contemporary matters of politics or art, with questions of peace or war, with persons or practices disliked by the comic writer. Occasionally the playwright used mythological material as a framework for his satire, but usually he invented his own plots, and often referred to contemporary persons or situations. The allusions were no doubt a source of considerable pleasure to the audiences of the day, but they are often obscure to a modern reader.

Numerous authors wrote Old Comedy, as the plays prior to 400 B.C. are called, but works by only one—Aristophanes (c. 448–380)—have survived. Aristophanes wrote about forty plays, of which eleven are extant: *The Acharnians* (425), *The Knights* (424), *The Clouds* (423), *The Wasps* (422), *Peace* (421), *The Birds* (414), *Lysistrata* (411), *Thesmophoriazusae* (411), *The Frogs* (405), *Ecclesiazusae* (392 or 391), and *Plutus* (388). Aristophanes began competing in the contests in 427, and though he may have acted in a few of his plays, he usually depended on others to produce his works.

His comedies mingle farce, personal abuse, fantasy, beautiful lyric

A redrawing from a vase painting of a type of costume probably used for tragedy in the fifth century B.C.

poetry, literary and musical parody, and serious commentary on contemporary affairs. Here *The Clouds* will be examined in some detail as an example of Aristophanes' work. It was produced at the City Dionysia in 423 B.C. and was awarded the third prize. Aristophanes later revised the script, but it is unclear how the present version differs from the original.

The Clouds

Themes and Ideas. The dominant idea of *The Clouds* is the corrupting influence of the Sophists, in whose teachings Aristophanes saw a danger to Athenian values. The Sophists were interested in rhetoric and argumentation, but, because they were skeptical of absolute values, to Aristophanes they appeared more anxious to win contests than to defend valid positions.

While Socrates was not a Sophist, he was probably the most colorful figure among the teachers of that time. Aristophanes did not pretend to present Socrates' ideas accurately, but used him to epitomize the Sophistic teacher. Nor are the ideas of the Sophists truthfully represented; they too are altered for comic purposes.

The satire is directed at two aspects of Sophism: its methods and its effects. The scenes in the school are concerned with the first of these, while the evasion of obligations and Phidippides' treatment of his father are designed to show the latter.

Plot and Structure. The plot of an Old Comedy usually revolves around a "happy idea" and the results of putting it into practice. In *The Clouds*, the idea is conceived that paying debts can be avoided by using the "wrong logic" of Sophistic learning. After much ridicule of its methods, the new learning is put into practice with the anticipated results. But while it is effective in ridding Strepsiades of his debtors, it has also taught his son, Phidippides, to beat and abuse him.

Structurally, Old Comedy follows a typical pattern composed of these elements: a *prologue*, during which the happy idea is conceived; the *parodos*, or entry of the chorus; the *agon*, or debate over the merits of the idea, ending with a decision to adopt it; the *parabasis*, a choral passage addressed to the audience and most frequently filled with advice on civic or other contemporary problems; a *series of episodes* showing the happy idea put into practice; and the *komos*, or exit to feasting and general revelry. Although all of the usual structural features are present in *The Clouds*, they have been rearranged. The deviations will be noted in the discussion which follows.

In the prologue to *The Clouds*, Strepsiades sets forth his predicament in a straightforward expository monologue. He is heavily in debt because of the extravagances of his son, Phidippides. He concludes that the only solution is to send his son to Socrates' school to learn how to avoid paying the debts. When Phidippides refuses to attend school, Strepsiades decides to go himself. The scene shifts instantly from Strepsiades' house to Socra-

Production photograph of The Clouds *as presented in 1951 by the Greek National Theatre. (Reproduced by permission.)*

tes' school. A number of satirical and farcical jokes about the school and its students concludes the prologue.

The parodos follows. Like many Greek comedies, *The Clouds* takes its title from the chorus, which frequently, as it does here, points up the element of fantasy. The clouds represent the spirit of the new learning which leads men on and then punishes them. The opening song also illustrates the element of lyrical poetry for which Aristophanes is noted.

Usually the agon follows the parodos, but in *The Clouds* an episode is introduced to ridicule additional aspects of the new learning. This episode is followed by the parabasis, which denounces the audience for not properly appreciating Aristophanes' merits. He unashamedly praises himself and ridicules his opponents.

The parabasis is followed by still another episode showing Strepsiades' inability to absorb the new learning. This episode implies that a man brought up in the old straight-laced ways of Athens cannot really understand the subtleties of the new way. After a choral ode, Strepsiades finally forces Phidippides to attend Socrates' school.

At this point, the long-delayed agon, or debate, occurs. The participants are personifications of Right Logic and Wrong Logic, another example of the fantasy that is typical of Old Comedy. As is usual, at the end of the agon all of the characters agree upon a line of action; here it is decided that Phidippides will be educated in the tradition of Wrong Logic.

This decision is followed by a short second parabasis, directed to the judges of the contest, suggesting that Aristophanes should win the prize.

Time passes very rapidly in the next thirty-five lines, for at that point Phidippides reenters having already completed his training.

A series of episodes showing the results of Strepsiades' plan follows: The creditors appear one by one and are effectively silenced. Strepsiades is overjoyed with his success and leads Phidippides away for feasting and revelry. This exist constitutes the komos and would normally conclude the play.

The joy is short-lived, however, for after a brief choral ode Strepsiades reappears, having been beaten by Phidippides, who then proves by the lesson learned from Wrong Logic that it is his duty to punish his father. The play ends as Strepsiades, in a fit of rage and frustration, attempts to burn Socrates' school. Such an ending is atypical of Old Comedy, for as a rule joy and harmony prevail.

The unity of Old Comedy is to be found in its ruling idea rather than in a sequence of causally related events. Consequently, its structure often seems haphazard. The episodes which show the idea being put into practice are especially apt to appear disconnected. The order could be rearranged and the number of episodes could be increased or reduced without seriously altering the story. They do build in comic intensity, however, and they carry out the author's purpose effectively.

The treatment of time and place in *The Clouds* is dictated by dramatic needs without any attempt at creating an illusion of reality. Sometimes hours or days are assumed to have passed during one or two speeches, and the place changes at will. Stage illusion is broken frequently: the characters make comments about the audience, and the chorus addresses the spectators directly in the parabasis.

The element of fantasy can be seen in both the personification of the clouds and in the exaggeration of ideas and situations. Thus, while the incidents are related to contemporary affairs, they are treated through the techniques of the "tall story."

Characters and Acting. Aristophanes' plays seem to indicate that all men are governed by materialistic and biological instincts and are in part corrupt and selfish. That Aristophanes held this opinion of his audience as well is suggested by his frequent practice of implying that the adoption of his point of view will bring monetary and sexual rewards.

Old Comedy puts much more emphasis on the physical aspects of characterization than tragedy does. Aristophanes' major characters are usually drawn from the well-to-do landowners (comparable to the middle class today), while the minor characters are either members of the same class or slaves. Occasionally heroes or gods appear, but they are always brought down to the level of ordinary human beings by emphasizing their materialistic and selfish instincts.

Typically, the main character in a play by Aristophanes is the common man, but one who is worse than the average audience member considers himself to be. Although any comedy may arouse a feeling of superiority,

Aristophanes puts this response to special use. Because he wants reform, he makes it seem possible by letting the members of the audience feel that they are wiser than the characters in the play.

Aristophanes' characters are never villainous, merely ridiculous. Rather than focusing attention upon the moral nature of the "idea," he emphasizes the ludicrous or happy results of adopting it. Thus, the characters are usually concerned with expediency—how well a plan can serve their own purposes—rather than with moral implications. Strepsiades, for example, never considers the moral implications of cheating his creditors, only the means by which it can be done. But, although the moral issues are never allowed to become the center of his plays, Aristophanes never lets the audience forget that the situations have wider and more important applications. Again, he achieves his purpose in part by allowing his audience to feel morally superior to the characters.

The acting style emphasized the physical, ridiculous, and ordinary details of everyday life. For example, at the opening of *The Clouds*, Strepsiades and Phidippides, wraped in blankets, are snoring; Strepsiades awakens and sends for a lamp and his account books. Later the characters catch bedbugs, beat each other, and climb onto the roof.

Old Comedy is as far removed from tragedy as possible; it ridicules man for giving into his materialistic and petty instincts, whereas tragedy empathizes with man's attempt to rise above those instincts. Thus, comic acting was probably no more realistic than that in tragedy; its deviation

Scene from Greek New Comedy. Drawing of a bas relief. (From Pougin, Dictionnaire, *1885.)*

from normal behavior was in a different direction, for it ridicules some aspects of human behavior just as tragic acting dignified others.

Setting, Spectacle, Dance, and Music. *The Clouds* demands a more complex setting and shows more clearly the facilities of the Greek theatre than *Oedipus the King* does. One interior and two exterior scenes are indicated. The interior was probably suggested by the *eccyclema*, while the two exteriors could be distinguished by the widely separated doors of the *skene*. The *machina* and the roof of the scene house were also used.

Many of the jokes in *The Clouds* are "sight gags." For example, Socrates is suspended in the machine (usually reserved for the gods) to indicate the pretentiousness and essential impracticality of the new learning. Other elements of note include the cloud costumes of the chorus, the grotesque and ludicrously obscene appearance of other characters, and the lively music and dance.

Thus, Old Comedy is a theatrical form of varied appeal. It is a strange mixture of fantasy, farce, and poetry which celebrates man's instincts while implicitly demanding that he act rationally. It is the reverse side of the coin of which tragedy is the face. Together comedy and tragedy indicate the range of the Greek view of man.

Late Greek Drama

Aristophanes was the last important exponent of Old Comedy. Furthermore, since all the great tragic dramatists were gone by the time he died in 380 B.C., Greek drama declined markedly in quality, if not in quantity, during the fourth century. Nevertheless, the theatre continued to expand, both in geographical distribution and in popularity.

In the fourth century, the Macedonians overran Greece. Their leader, Alexander the Great, then went on to conquer Asia Minor and northern Africa. Since the Greeks had already established colonies in southern Italy and Sicily, by the end of the fourth century almost all of the Mediterranean area had been "Hellenized." Pergamum (in Asia Minor) and Alexandria (in Egypt) soon rivaled Athens as centers of learning. Wherever the Greek influence was felt, theatres were built.

Although the taste for tragedy continued, comedy was the preferred form. But the comedy which satisfied this taste was not that of Aristophanes, for citizens were no longer free to ridicule their rulers or to demand reforms. Athens and other Greek territories were now ruled by despots. The New Comedy (as it is usually called) which amused these people is most intimately associated with Menander (c. 342–292 B.C.), a native of Athens. He is said to have written over one hundred comedies of which only one, *The Grouch* (rediscovered in 1957) remains in its entirety. Substantial portions of several other plays (*The Woman of Samos, The Shield, The Arbitration,* and *She Who Was Shorn*) also have been recovered.

A reconstruction of the Hellenistic theatre at Oropos. Painted panels could be set between the columns below, while some scenic representation may have been used in the alcoves at the rear of the raised stage. (From Ernst Fiechter, Antike Griechische Theaterbauten, *courtesy Verlag W. Kohlhammer GmbH.)*

New Comedy was divided into five parts by four choral interludes. By this time, however, the chorus was of little importance and served merely to break the play into scenes. But the major change was in subject matter, which was now drawn from the everyday life of middle-class Athenians. The plays were light in tone and perhaps most typically showed a son's attempt to marry in spite of his father's opposition. The son was usually aided by a clever slave, who was the major source of humor. Eventually the father was reconciled to the son's choice, frequently because the girl was discovered to be the long-lost child of a friend.

New Comedy used costumes which were reasonsly close copies of everyday garments, and masks which depicted basic character types of the period. Altogether, it marked a movement toward realism in staging, and toward conventionalization in depicting human behavior.

At the same time, the staging of tragedy moved further away from realism. It is to the period after 336 (usually called the Hellenistic age) that the distorted masks, high headdresses, thick-soled boots, and padded bodies of tragic actors belong. New theatres were built with stages raised from eight to thirteen feet above the level of the orchestra. The actor became increasingly the center of interest as he performed on this new stage high above the orchestra. Plays now ceased to be produced exclusively at the Dionysian festivals and were given on many other civic or religious occasions.

As the fondness for theatrical performances grew, the demand for trained personnel became so great that performers organized the Artists of Dionysus, which supplied towns with the actors, trainers for choruses, musicians, and other personnel needed for the production of plays. It set fees for services, and its rights were recognized by international agreement. Many of its members were exempt from military service, had freedom of travel, and sometimes served as ambassadors between states.

In the third century B.C. Rome began to expand as a power and came into contact with the theatre for the first time. As it absorbed the Hellenic world, it took over the theatre and transformed it in accordance with its own needs. The distinctively Greek theatre had almost disappeared by the second century B.C., and from then until the sixth century A.D. the theatre was to be principally a Roman institution.

5
Roman Theatre and Drama

Tradition has it that Rome was founded in the eighth century B.C. At first a small town of little consequence, it did not begin to assume prominence until the third century B.C. But by the beginning of the Christian era it had extended its power over most of the then known world. The Romans were remarkable for their ability to assimilate whatever attracted them elsewhere. Thus, when they found drama in the Greek colonies in Sicily and southern Italy, they imported it to Rome.

Long before regular drama was introduced, however, other types of theatrical entertainment were well established in Rome. Around 364 B.C., in an attempt to appease the gods when a plague was ravishing the city, musical and dancing performances were imported from neighboring Etruria and thereafter flourished. From the Etruscans the Romans also borrowed chariot racing, boxing, and gladiatorial contests, all of which were to be presented alongside drama, creating the circuslike atmosphere that surrounded theatre in Rome.

The first regular comedy and tragedy, by Livius Andronicus, a Greek from southern Italy, were presented in 240 B.C. Soon native-born authors

112

were writing plays, and the Greek form of drama had been naturalized in Rome.

Although a vast number of plays were written in Rome, works by only three dramatists survive: twenty-one comedies by Plautus, six comedies by Terence, and nine tragedies by Seneca. The comedies of Plautus and Terence date from about 205 to 160 B.C., the tragedies of Seneca from the first century A.D.

Roman Festivals

The *ludi,* or festivals, at which plays were performed in Rome, were not associated with the worship of Dionysus, but were of various types. Most were official religious celebrations, but some were financed by wealthy citizens for special occasions, such as the funeral of a distinguished figure or the triumphal entry of a victorious army. At first drama was given only at the *ludi Romani*, or Roman Games, and was probably restricted to a single day. But the popularity of dramatic entertainments insured their gradual expansion, and as the number of Roman festivals was increased so were the occasions for presenting plays. By 78 B.C., 48 days each year were devoted to dramatic entertainments at religious festivals. By A.D. 354, there were 175 public festival days of which 101 were devoted to theatrical spectacles.

Scene from a Roman comedy. After a wall painting in Pompeii. (From Navarre, Dionysos, *1895.)*

In the time of Plautus and Terence (the second century B.C.), plays were given principally at four festivals: the *ludi Romani,* held in September, with at least four days devoted to drama; the *ludi Plebeii,* established in 220 B.C. held in November, with at least three days given over to plays; the *ludi Apollinares,* begun in 212 B.C. and held in July, with approximately two days devoted to drama; and the *ludi Megalenses,* initiated in 204 B.C. and held in April, with six days of theatrical entertainments.

All state-financed festivals were religious celebrations in honor of the gods, but the Romans were more concerned with the letter than the spirit of the celebration. They believed that each festival, to be effective, must be carried through according to prescribed rules and that any mistake necessitated the repetition of the entire festival, including the plays. Since such repetitions were frequent, many more days were devoted to drama than might be supposed.

As in Greece, production expenses were undertaken by the state or by wealthy citizens. The Senate made an appropriation for each festival as a whole, and frequently the officials in charge contributed additional funds. These officials normally contracted for productions with the managers of theatrical companies, who then were responsible for all details of production: finding scripts, providing actors, musicians, costumes, and so on. Although each manager was assured of a certain sum of money, special incentives were provided in the form of prizes for the most successful troupes. The manager probably bought the play script outright from the author; it then remained the manager's property and might be played as often as he wished or as audiences demanded.

Admission was free to everyone, seats were not reserved, audiences were unruly, and no refreshments were available in the auditorium. Composed of a series of plays, the programs were lengthy; and, since the plays often had to compete with rival attractions, the troupes were forced to provide a kind of entertainment that would satisfy a mass audience.

The Theatre and Stage
in the Time of Plautus and Terence

Besides paying basic production expenses, the state supplied the theatre in which plays were presented. In the time of Plautus and Terence, it was a temporary one, for no permanent theatre was built in Rome until 55 B.C. Since plays were given in connection with religious festivals, each of which honored a specific god, and because each god had his own precinct and temple, it is likely that at each festival a theatre was set up near the temple of the god being honored.

Current ideas of the features of the early theatre are derived largely from the extant stone structures. Most of the surviving theatres, however, date from the first century A.D. or later, and do not necessarily provide an accurate picture of the temporary structures.

The theatre of Plautus and Terence probably included temporary scaffolds (outlining a semicircular orchestra) which provided seating for the spectators, and a long narrow stage rising about five feet above the orchestra level (the existing stages are over one hundred feet long), which was bounded by the stage house at the back and ends.

The appearance of the stage background, called the *scaenae frons*, is disputed. Some think that it was a flat wall upon which columns, statues, or other details were painted. Others believe that there were three-dimensional niches and porticoes and, for evidence, point to the many scenes in Roman comedy which require one character to remain unseen by others, even though all are on stage at the same time. This is not a wholly convincing argument, however, because stage convention in almost every period has permitted characters to see each other or not as the dramatic situation demands and has not depended on the use of places that would be considered adequate for concealment in real life. The back wall of the stage probably contained three openings, each of which might be treated, in comedy, as the entrance to a house. The stage then became a street, and the entrances at either end of the stage were assumed to be continuations of that street. Since windows and a second story are also required by some comedies, the background must have provided these as well.

Costumes and Masks for Comedy

Costumes in the Roman theatre varied with the type of play. The works of Plautus and Terence were adapted from Greek New Comedy and retained the Greek setting and garments. Other playwrights, however, wrote of Roman characters, and the costumes varied accordingly. In either case, the costumes were similar to those of daily life, although those of the more ludicrous comic characters were perhaps exaggerated.

Since most of the characters in Roman comedy were "types," the costumes also became standardized. There is evidence to suggest that certain colors were associated with particular occupations, such as yellow with courtesans and red with slaves. This conventional use of color extended to wigs as well. All of the actors wore masks, which made the doubling of parts much easier and simplified the casting of such roles as the identical twins in *The Menaechmi*. Each actor in comedy also wore a thin sandal or slipper, called a *soccus*.

Comic Playwrights

Although there were numerous comic writers in Rome, works by only two—Plautus and Terence—have survived. Titus Maccius Plautus (c. 224–

184 B.C.) is the earliest Roman playwright whose works still exist. Innumerable plays have been attributed to him, but the titles of only twenty-one have been agreed upon, all of which survive. The oldest dates from about 205 and the last from about the time of Plautus' death. Some of his most famous works are: *Amphitryon, The Pot of Gold, The Captives, The Braggart Warrior,* and *The Twin Menaechmi.*

Publius Terentius Afer, commonly called Terence, was born in 195 (some accounts say 185) and died in 159 B.C. A native of North Africa, he was brought to Rome as a slave, was later freed, and became the friend of many of the great men of his day. He wrote only six plays, all of which still exist: *The Woman of Andros, The Self-Tormenter, The Eunuch, Phormio, The Mother-in-Law,* and *The Brothers.*

The Conventions of Roman Comedy

The existing Roman comedies are adapted from Greek New Comedy. In this process of adaptation, the following changes seem to have been made (although so few New Comedies have survived that conclusions must be tentative). First, the chorus has been abandoned, doing away with the division of the texts into acts or scenes. (The divisions found in most modern editions were made in later times.) Second, the musical elements formerly associated with the chorus have been scattered throughout the plays: In some respects a Roman comedy resembled a modern musical, since certain scenes were spoken, others were recited to musical accompaniment, and a number of songs might be included. In Plautus' plays about two-thirds of the lines were accompanied by music, and the average number of songs was three. Although Terence did not use songs, music accompanied approximately half of his dialogue.

Roman comedy, like Greek New Comedy, is concerned not with political and social problems but with everyday domestic affairs. Almost invariably the plots turn on misunderstandings of one sort or another: mistaken identity (frequently involving long lost children), misunderstood motives, or deliberate deception. Sometimes the misunderstanding leads to farce, as in most of Plautus' plays, but it may also be used for sentimental effects, as when Terence emphasizes the problems of lovers or parent-child relationships.

Plautus typically employs a single plot and a complicated intrigue. In an expository prologue he explains the dramatic situation, and then he develops the farcical possibilities of the situation in the episodes that follow. Terence, on the other hand, uses a double plot, dispenses with the expository prologue, and treats his characters with sympathy and delicacy. His plays may be classified as romantic comedies, whereas those of Plautus are usually comedies of situation or farces.

Roman comedy deals with the affairs of the well-to-do middle class, and

Terra cotta of a Roman comic figure, The Thief (British Museum, Castellam Collection; print from Culver Pictures.)